THE AUTHOR

MYRON S. AUGSBURGER was born in 1929 at Elida, Ohio. He received the A.B. and Th.B. degrees from Eastern Mennonite College, Harrisonburg, Va., the B.D. degree from Goshen College Biblical Seminary, Goshen, Ind., and the Th.M. and Th.D. degrees from Union Theological Seminary, Richmond, Va. He was ordained to the ministry in 1951, as pastor of the Tuttle Avenue Mennonite Church, Sarasota, Florida. For four years he was pastor of students at Eastern Mennonite College. In January, 1964, he was appointed president-elect of Eastern Mennonite College.

He has served with great effectiveness as an evangelist, both in congregational meetings and in community crusades, which are sponsored by Inter-Church Evangelism, Inc., of Atglen, Pennsylvania. This ministry has taken him through much of the United States and Canada and into numerous foreign countries. His community crusades are conducted in tents, arenas, or city auditoriums, and usually under interdenominational auspices.

He is author of *Called to Maturity* (1960) and *Quench Not the Spirit* (1962).

INVITATION
TO
DISCIPLESHIP

The Message of Evangelism

By

Myron S. Augsburger

HERALD PRESS, SCOTTDALE, PENNSYLVANIA

To my parents

Clarence and Estella Augsburger

From whom I first learned of Christ

PREFACE

This book of meditations on evangelism is written from the background of having served as a pastor with an evangelistic program, of having studied systematic theology with the intent of deepening the content in evangelistic work, of the benefits of having taught various college and seminary courses in evangelism, and above all, of having served as evangelist in scores of evangelistic crusades (congregational and city-wide interchurch meetings) in the past ten years. Many of the ideas presented in this work have been gleaned from the valuable lessons that have come to me in the preaching mission of evangelism, while other lessons have come by the multiple and enriching experiences of sharing with pastors of many denominations in co-operative crusades, by studying the work of evangelists, past and contemporary, by sitting under professors from whom I occasionally quote in this work, and by reading widely in the field in Christian literature. This book is written to share, not to pose as having all the answers, but to offer arguments as to how the Gospel is the answer. My theological presuppositions can be clearly seen throughout the book, for every man presents his understanding of Christ from his own orientation and study. Although this work is not primarily a treatment of method, the author considers mass evangelism as valid as any method, and would affirm that where evangelistic preaching has theological depth the preaching mission is as valid in communicating at the grass roots of the church as is higher education in communicating to a select group. Methods are not under question as much as content; if the content is rich enough, the method will be both directed and judged by the content. The Christian church needs to move among men, until feeling their pulse, heartaches, burdens, and sins there is born anew in the heart of the church a spirit of true compassion. Strange as it may seem, however, the person most severely criticized within the Christian church is invariably the one who seeks to befriend sinners!

—Myron S. Augsburger

CONTENTS

1

THE CHURCH
IN MISSION

"Now then we are ambassadors for Christ. . . ." *II Corinthians 5:20*

Evangelism is the life of the church. The only means of growth in the church of Christ is by the conversion of sinners to the Lord. The church is composed of those who have entered a covenant relation of faith with the Lord of the universe. Our entering this covenant is by a faith response to the good news of the evangel. The church of Christ is thus by her very nature committed to the task of evangelism. The Lord of the church has placed before the believers a mission: "Go ye therefore, and teach all nations" (Matt. 28:19), or with the force of the original language, while going about in your personal world, make disciples of all men.

The church, planted in a world influenced constantly by the demonic (Eph. 2:2), is commissioned by Christ to be on the offensive, moving into enemy territory to win persons to Him. The people of God are called to resist the demonic on every front, to move forward in areas where the darkness is most intense, knowing that "the gates of hell shall not prevail" (Matt. 16:18) against the church. Too often the church has failed to be evangelistic because it has been on the defensive rather than the offensive. The

9

church has often been more concerned to prove itself right than to present the message which by its transforming effect is its own proof. The mission of the church has too often been handled much like a man planting a tree and building a fence around it for its protection, then spending most of his time keeping up the fence. The church is to be a conscience to society, a witness against the unbelief that rejects Christ, a bulwark of integrity in a world of decaying morals, but the church must be this and more by a positive contribution to society. Any program that can negate more clearly than it can affirm has lost its power. Jesus said that the Christian is to be "in the world" at the same time as he is "not of the world" (John 17:11-16). Too frequently the church has either been of the world and lost its witness by compromise, or it has withdrawn to avoid being of the world and thereby failed to be in the world with a creative witness.

I. Evangelism is letting people know and persuading them to accept the Gospel. It is the persuasive presentation of faith in Christ. Its methods are multiple, but its purpose is singular—inviting individuals to enter a faith relation with the Lord Christ. It may be by life—by behaving according to one's belief; it may be by announcement—by teaching or preaching for commitment. But if it is truly evangelism the method is subservient to the witness. The Gospel, the invitation to personal relation with the person of the risen Christ, can always be made relevant to persons of every class and race.

The task of theology is that of interpreting intelligently and intelligibly the Christian message of the saving Person and His principles. This message has come to us in the revelation of events and in the interpretations of the Spirit. This task cannot be done in an ivory tower, for theology is part of the mission of the church. Consequently it is a mistake to conclude that theology and evangelism are at odds; rather, it must be affirmed that either one is incomplete without the other.

Evangelism that is only a play on the emotions or psychological hungers of the self, rather than a depth experience of what it means to stand in humble surrender before the Thou of the universe, is inadequate. We are in need of evangelism in depth, a new awareness of what it means to bring the whole of life under the lordship of Christ. On the other hand, an armchair theology that only philosophizes about the issues of polemics or apologetics stops short of the goal of theology. Genuine theology is dynamic not static. It is the interpretation of the supernatural in a manner that witnesses to what God has done and is doing in history. Christianity is rooted in history, the record of a God who acts; and as such, theology is the attempt to explain what is happening in the God-man relationship. And "real" history is salvation history—the rest is only a spinning of wheels.

The church, to be consistent with its essential nature, must continue to demonstrate by this witness-character of discipleship that the lordship of the risen Christ is a reality. It is in evangelism that the believers declare their place as subjects before Him who is both contemporary and Lord. Whether this is done in worship or by a witness that takes Christ out of the church into the world, the declaration of Christ's lordship and our discipleship must be made. As Brunner has said, "The church exists by mission as fire exists by burning." The church is only truly the church when souls are being saved through its witness to Christ. As Christians, the work of the kingdom is our primary mission, and this is a redemptive mission, filling up in our bodies the suffering of the Lord Jesus by sharing the hostility of unbelievers against the Christ. Col. 1:24.

II. Evangelism is the announcement of the kerygma. The Gospel tells of a God who acts, involving Himself in man's problems and moving to us in grace, producing spiritual wholeness. Christianity makes more sense out of life than any philosophy that is compared with it, for Christianity is a personalistic faith which reconciles our person to the ultimate Person and interprets life in a manner consistent with its basic purpose of fellowship with God. The only "real" man this world has ever seen was Jesus Christ, for in Him we discover what God originally purposed for man. Likewise, through Him we enter a new life in which the Spirit of God works that we may be conformed to the image of His dear Son. Rom. 8:29. Consequently, the proclamation of the kerygma is a call for conversion, a change of direction that brings our perversity and rebellion to a halt and introduces us into a new life of fellowship with God in Christ.

The Christian message is the most relevant of all announcements to a modern world. It is not a naive faith, nor is it simply offering "pie in the sky" for tomorrow, nor is it simply insurance that one will escape hell and gain heaven! The Christian message calls one to a creative fellowship with God as modern as tomorrow; it introduces one to a quality of life here and now. A spiritual birth introduces one to a wholly new dimension of life; it satisfies the deepest longings of one's true being for identity with ultimate reality by fellowship with a personal God. Modern man finds his life characterized by loneliness, and Christian faith answers by fellowship and brotherhood; by frustration, and Christianity answers with security and hope; by relativity in moral ideals, and Christianity answers with the norm of Christ; by despair, to be answered by eternal purpose and joy; by hostility, to be answered by forgiveness and peace; by sensuality, answered by wholeness and love; and by escapism, answered by an honest confession and a "new being." Christ offers wholeness for our fragmented lives, a wholeness that is the work of grace, the "power to become the sons of God" (John 1:12).

Evangelism is theology aflame. It is the witness of the transformed heart. It is the call to share life in Christ. It is the winning of estranged souls back to their Lord and ours. Evangelism is the persuasive influence of the soul satisfied with his Christ.

2

THE PRIMACY OF THE
IN-CHRIST EXPERIENCE

"Therefore if any man be in Christ,
he is a new creature: old things are passed away; behold,
all things are become new." II Corinthians 5:17

The Christian faith stands in contrast to, rather than in comparison with, the other religions of the world. It is not simply a call to be religious, nor is it an announcement of ethical principles; but it is rather the self-disclosure of God in Christ, inviting us to fellowship with Him. Confronted with a person we are never neutral; we either give that person acceptance or rejection. It follows that the question of being a Christian is not simply a moralistic one, but personalistic. It is a question of opening one's life to the God who would share it with us. God has come to us —we have no alternative but to do something with Him—we either accept or reject Him.

One of the most frequent expressions in the writing of the Apostle Paul is his phrase "in Christ." To be in Christ is to be a new creature, to have brought a vertical dimension into one's life that transforms the horizontal. To be "in Christ" is a relationship as real as that involved in matrimony. As marriage means the radical reorientation of the individual's life to share fully with another, just so being "in Christ" is a spiritual reorientation of one's whole life. A sinner is a self-oriented person, while a Christian is a Christ-oriented person. There is no neutrality about the question of marriage: either you are married or you aren't. Just so, there is no neutrality about being in Christ: either you are committed to Christ or you aren't.

The claim of Christianity is that Jesus Christ is God. This means that we do not think of Him as another in a series of prophets telling us about God, nor simply as a man who had a greater consciousness of God than any previous man has had, nor even that He is one who is like God. Rather, the Bible tells us that no man has seen God at any time. John 1:18. He is the "hidden One," yet He has revealed Himself to us in Christ. Paul writes that God was in Christ, reconciling the world unto Himself. II Cor. 5:20. Should one endeavor to take a superior position of complimenting Christ by saying He is like God, the question could and should immediately be asked, "How do you know what God is like, that you can say of Jesus that He is *like* God?" Actually the Christian is one who beholding Jesus experiences a dawning of faith that says, "So this is what God is like!" Either Jesus Christ was God or we have not had a full and valid revelation. When we say that God meets us in Jesus Christ, we are affirming that no one can conceive of God fully except as He is known in Christ, and no one can come to God except through the revelation He has made of Himself in Christ.

This faith is the scandal of the Gospel, the offense of the cross, the stumbling block to many. This is the exclusiveness of the Christian message, for if God has met us in Christ, all other religions that speak about God are inadequate and judged as incomplete by the Christian faith. God as person, God as love, God with a "face" is only known in Christ. Jesus said, "He that hath seen me hath seen the Father" (John 14:9). But many have not seen Him, for blinded by the materialism of human thought they have only seen the man Jesus and missed seeing the real Man, the God-Man within the human form. Jesus told Nicodemus that just as Israel experienced healing by looking at the brazen serpent on the pole, and that away and beyond that form on the pole stood

Jehovah God who heals, so man's salvation comes by looking at a form on a cross and finding in faith that beyond that form of man there was the very God of heaven who had come to redeem man. John 3:14-17.

Man in sin, the perversion of the good, needs to discover that God cares, and cares deeply enough to involve Himself in man's problem for correction. In history the extent of this perversion was laid bare at the cross, where man in his hostility sought to remove God rather than relate to Him in love. Currently man's perversion is seen not only in moral degeneracy but in the indifference toward God that ignores Him. In fact, it may be said that the sin of modern man is worse than that of those who crucified Jesus: they at least paid Him the respect of noticing Him, of reacting to His holiness, while the modern world stoops so low as to ignore Him, as though to say, "Who is Jesus that we should even notice Him?"

We live in a world that is precarious: no doubt God permitted it to become that way so man wouldn't find his security here. Yet man continues to talk as though God owes him a good world in which he can indulge in his selfishness. He attacks the idea of God with a bitterness that cries out, "Where is God? If He exists, why doesn't He straighten out the mess this old world is in?" We may rightly ask to what end: so that man can indulge his selfishness? Man is asking the wrong question: he ought to be asking, "What is God trying to tell us through this mess?" God is showing us that this is the kind of world that results from man shoving God out of his life! The answer to the question of God's ability to create wholeness is found only in Christ: it is the wholeness of a satisfying life in Him rather than God becoming man's little bellhop to enable him to live selfishly. Col. 1:19, 20.

I. *Personalism, Rather Than Moralism,*
   Is the Key to the Christian Faith

Christianity is the self-disclosure of a personal God, and Christian experience is a faith-relation with a person—Christ. Gal. 2:20. Evangelism is not simply announcing a new philosophy, nor introducing a new system of ethics. Our tendencies toward moralism cut the nerve of evangelistic response. The dynamic of faith is in the call to fellowship, and this is superior to the static call to idolize a system of faith. Christ is greater than any system of religion or structure of doctrine. He is all that our doctrines say about Him, but He is more than that. The doctrines of the Christian church have grown up as the expressions and interpretations of what it means to be "in Christ." Out of this transforming experience men have written to interpret and communicate their knowledge of Him.

Far too often the evangelistic activities of the church are simply a stirring over again of the same people. Instead of being fishers of men we are keepers of aquariums, and flatter ourselves when we have "stolen fish" from someone else's bowl. Many churches have grown up around some personality or pet doctrine purely by proselyting or division, while in the New Testament churches grew up by building converts from paganism into a brotherhood of believers. We need to remind ourselves that no group has captured the kingdom, and that our work is that of bearing witness to what Christ is doing through His Spirit.

The problem is augmented for the contemporary church by the fact that there are many church members who have never been converted, who have never entered a personal relationship with Christ. Dr. E. Stanley Jones says that two thirds of the members of the professing Christian church have never been converted. He quotes the archbishops' report as saying, "The church is a field for evangelism rather than a force." Multitudes of professing Christians have a secondhand or a borrowed religion. Madam Cherkoff of Russia, when asked about her relation to God answered, "Ask my father confessor, I pay him for that." So many would leave the issue of their personal relation to Christ in the hands of their pastor or answer it with the vagueness of their corporate involvement in Christendom. This is heresy in comparison with Paul's testimony, "For to me to live is Christ" (Phil. 1:21), "I am crucified with Christ: nevertheless I live, yet not I, but Christ liveth in me" (Gal. 2:20).

Christian faith is the most personal thing in the world. God in grace singles out the individual with the awareness that we count with God, that He cares. Here one discovers the greatest sense of personal worth, of the value of personality, to be known in life. With the awareness of a heart that is perverse, of a life that has closed God out, we discover that our problems are not simply moralistic but personalistic. We are persons that like sin, that like to go our own way.

The problems that we have are the fruit of the problem that we are. This is the real problem that Christ came to correct. He didn't just come to save us from the problems that we have, He came to save us from the problem that we are! Isa. 53:6. The saving of a soul is the saving of the whole person, not a little entity down inside of us. Man is a living soul, a unitary being, and in his salvation the whole life is brought under the lordship of Christ. Evangelism calls one into a saving relationship. It is the making of disciples. It is turning people from darkness to light, from rebellion to surrender, from estrangement to fellowship. I John 1:7.

II. *The Imperative of the I-Thou Rather Than the I-It Stance*

Christianity is the revelation of a God who acts. It is a message rooted in history, the record of the mighty acts of God for the redemption of His creation. This unfolding of divine purpose presented in the Scripture finds its culmination in Christ, in His birth-death-rising again and in the promise of His return. The acts of God give purpose and meaning to history. Apart from this, man is only caught up in a cycle. Outside of the eschatological hope of the Scripture secular history is only spinning its wheels. The historian interprets from a given stance: should he interpret history in A.D. 30 he could begin with the Orient, or with Julius Caesar, or with Jesus of Nazareth. Where he begins makes all the difference in his system of historical interpretation. The Christian begins with Christ rather than Caesar.

Evangelism is thus the relating of saving events in the self-disclosure of God, primarily the ultimate event of the work of Christ. We are telling a story more than proving an insight—a story of the acts of God. We are bringing to contemporary man

an awareness that he stands before the God of the universe, before
the contemporary Christ, and under the impact of the convicting
Spirit. God is at work in this world, taking out of the world a
people for His name. Acts 15:14. The conviction that the universe
is permeated with the Divine Person and purpose calls one to a
stance that is different from simply answering to a philosophy or
system of religion. Man stands before the Thou of the universe,
not before an it or an object of religious thought. Ex. 20:2, 3.

In our tendency to idolize science, and to take a stance of
subject analyzing the object, the challenge of existentialism is a
needed corrective. Granting that humanistic existentialism is bank-
rupt when compared with divine revelation, it has served to under-
mine the humanistic idolizing of science. Science is never limited
to the realm of analysis. The scientist begins with faith premises,
makes observations, analyzes data, and presents an interpretation.
Thus ultimately he becomes a philosopher! Science is thus a method, not a master. Martin Buber has called our contemporary
world to an awareness that in contemplation of God we do not
stand as the subject before the object, as the I before the it.
Rather, we stand in awe before the Thou of the universe. He is the
Subject and we become aware of a new I-Thou relation that trans-
fixes our humanistic pride and calls us to response in worship.
Evangelism in the twentieth century should not only be cognizant
of this, but should find here a medium of communication that can
call men to personal awareness of answering to God. We must
make clear that God is His own proof, rather than let man think
he can prove or disprove God. Relation with God, like a relation
of love, must be experienced to be known, and when it is experienced, it is its own proof. One doesn't stand outside and try to
prove it, making the Thou an it, any more than a wife or husband
can prove the love of a companion. Should a detective be hired
to gather data and prove the companion's love, the very love itself
would be destroyed, for love is built on faith and confidence and
such an enterprise of proving it has already destroyed it. There
is much evidence, both on the level of love, between companions,
and of a personal God with whom one can relate, but the proof

itself is only by involvement and never in detachment.

The I-Thou awareness is also an evidence of the quality of the Christian faith. The pagan religions reveal that in their system the more religious a person becomes, the less personalistic, the less interested in history, and the less concerned about moral obligation. In Christianity the more spiritual a person becomes, the more deeply personalistic rather than legalistic he is, the more vitally interested in the working out of God's purpose in history, and the more conscientious about moral and ethical responsibility.

To be in Christ is to become a new being, to share a divine life and purpose, and to live with a sense of divine presence. A Christian is a Christ-indwelled person. The believer is a new creature because of a new presence and power in his life, transforming the whole person. Grace thus works an ontological change in the person's life, and through the regeneration of the Spirit life in Christ is now life in sanctification. Gal. 5:22-26.

III. *Conversion as "Knowledge of" Rather Than "Knowledge About" Christ*

Accepting the lower level of Christian thought in moralism rather than the higher level of personalism the Christian church has tended to minimize if not reject the experience of conversion. The impact of religious education has led many to think of becoming a Christian as something akin to graduation, in which one has gained enough knowledge about Christ to be called a Christian or a follower of Jesus. There are several mistakes implicit in this which it is the task of evangelism to expose and answer.

First, conversion is not a matter of growth in knowledge in the field of religion. It is a redirection, a turning around. One does not simply grow in knowledge about Christ and count himself a Christian. The light of truth to be received in Christian education reveals to man his own inner perversity and his self-centeredness. Confronting such an one with Jesus Christ he makes a choice between the way of self and the way of Christ. Conversion is a turning around, a renunciation of self and a confession of Christ as Lord, a radical change of control in one's life. Matt. 10:32-34.

Second, being a follower of Jesus is not simply imitation but identification with Him. One is not married by simply imitating the ideals and way of life of the person admired or loved but by sharing life in all its fullness. Being Christian is not simply copying Christ; it is committing the whole life to Him. We can't imitate Jesus adequately even when we try, for we are not another little Jesus—we are depraved, perverted, and sinful. Dr. Paul Shearer has said, "That is too much like showing the ostrich egg to a Bantam hen and saying, Look at that and do your best!" Being a disciple of Jesus Christ is not simply to imitate His life. It is to accept Him for all that He claimed to be, the Son of God and our Lord and Saviour; it is to come to Him through the way He Himself taught, in repentance of our sins, in a confession of His lordship, and in a discipleship of obedient service. If Christ is our Lord, then we are His subjects, and this relation is the correction of our rebellion and the entering into righteousness in Christ. Col. 3:1-3.

Third, conversion is a personal, existential involvement with Christ. By this is meant that Christian experience is not simply a "knowledge about" but is a "knowledge of" Christ. It is one thing to have a knowledge about marriage through having grown up in a family environment and by having studied writings about marriage and the family, but it is another thing to have a "knowledge of" marriage by being personally in love and having entered into marriage bonds with another. So there is a step from the level where Christian education has given us a knowledge about Christ into the knowledge of Christ as personal Lord and Saviour—a step of faith, a leap of faith, if you please. Evangelism is soliciting persons to take that step, to move beyond what they know "about," into the reality of the "in Christ" experience itself. Col. 1:27.

It is a tragedy when the Christian educator or pastor leads a person through all the catechetical instruction about Christ and stops short of inviting that person to go on beyond the "knowledge about" to the "knowledge of." But it must also be said that while the moralism of some has clouded over the Biblical call to conversion, the sacramentalism of others has done the same. Under this influence the individual is led to believe he is receiving grace in the sacraments that in turn secures his salvation, a salvation that is thought of as an I-it rather than an I-Thou. Sacramentalism obscures the personalism of Christian faith by moving the person further back, while it holds the symbol to the fore, and the concept of entering into a saving relationship here and now is lost. To place the focus of one's faith upon the sacraments is to idolize them and to insult the person who said, "This is my body." We need to make clear the meaning of Paul's words, "Though we have known Christ after the flesh, yet now henceforth know we him no more." The leap of faith, the trust in the "hidden One" who is risen Lord, can only be expressed by a personalistic involvement with Christ through the witness of His Spirit.

Fidelity to a person is never out of date: in this sense evangelism is one of the most relevant programs in the world, the call to a faith relation with Jesus Christ. Evangelism has too often been cheapened. On the sophisticated intellectual level it is often cheapened by interpreting Christian experience as merely the acceptance of Christian values. John 5:34-40. On the emotional level it has been cheapened by certain types of emotional experience rather than a deliberate faith-response to the truth as it is in Jesus. John 8:31-36. In the professional evangelistic activities it is often cheapened by manipulating people, by use of gimmicks or vagueness in an invitation that does not emphasize deep, honest response. I Cor. 2:1-5. True evangelism is the announcement of the good news of God's redemptive acts, the center of which is shown in the cross and the risen Christ. It is the solicitation of persons to yield their lives to Him and experience the regeneration of the Holy Spirit.

Salvation is to be "in Christ," to know His forgiveness and His deliverance from our sins and our selfishness. Evangelism is the call to relationship, to open one's life to God, to renounce the way of rebellion and to realize His redemptive presence. To be born again, to experience the beginning of personal spiritual life through Christ Jesus is the answer to the emptiness and perversion of man's life. Only in leading persons to this commitment have we fulfilled the commission "to make disciples of all men." Every Christian, going about in his personal world, whether it be the geographical world or the vocational world, is to so live Christ as to be giving an invitation to discipleship.

3

THE INTELLECTUAL CHALLENGE
OF FAITH

*"I am the way, the truth, and the
life, no one cometh unto the Father
but by me." John 14:6*

The Bible affirms that man was created in the image of God. A part of this image is man's ability to think, to reason, and to choose, to be creative and effective in his privilege of life, to love and fellowship. Christianity is a thinking man's religion. It is more than simply a process of thought, for it is the involvement of man's life with the divine person Himself. But the involvement is nevertheless one of communication, which means thought. The Christian faith has always been a challenge to great minds at the same time as it has been a ground of security for simple faith.

There are several difficulties, however, in the processes of Christian thought, among which must be mentioned the fact that philosophy without revelation is limited to this side of the line, that the field of the metaphysic must find its evidence in categories of faith rather than of modern science, and that the eternal cannot be bottled up in the systems of the temporal. Just as one cannot make a flat map of a round world and make it accurate, so one cannot bring the eternal into time and explain it all. Christianity is philosophy with a "given." The difficulties for the natural man do not rule out the Christian faith as illogical.

The scientist who says he cannot believe in God because he cannot accept a metaphysic is overlooking the fact that he cannot prove by science that there is no God. Consequently, his position of unbelief is a faith position. The atheist thus has a faith position, one that he cannot prove by science, when he affirms that there is no God. In comparison, the Christian has a faith position, a faith that there is a God who has revealed Himself. Both are faith positions. However, there is a tremendous amount of evidence that undergirds the "faith position" of the Christian and throws the burden of proof back upon the one who affirms the negative. The Christian can build a significant case to demonstrate that his faith position makes more sense out of life than any other contrary position.

Evangelism is the announcement that the Christian faith answers the questions concerning the ultimate meaning of life in a way that no humanistic philosophy can. Evangelism calls us to face the intellectual questions of our day with a humble assurance that the "truth is in Jesus" if we but find it. Dr. Glover of England said, "The early church grew because it out-thought, out-lived, and out-died everybody around it." As Paul poured new truth into the molds of the vocabulary and questions of his day, so we must pour Christian truth into the questions of our own time. Man's tendency, however, is to idolize his opinions and definitions and consequently he is rendered impotent when he wants to speak to those to whom his opinions do not communicate more than himself.

This tendency to idolatry has plagued the church from its birth. In the long period before the Reformation men were idolizing a system of religion. Although the work of Luther called men back to trust in Christ, the century following the Reformation was characterized by idolizing a system of doctrine. In reaction to this the world moved into the period of the enlightenment and made an idol out of man's reason. The logical consequence of this was in the ninteenth century's idolizing of "man" in anticipation of a golden age. And following two world wars, which God used to shatter man's faith in man, we have come to idolize modern science.

As George Buttrick has said, "It is too bad that modern science, the child of theology, has kicked its mother out-of-doors!"

Our generation, which has grown up with the findings of science before it, has overlooked the fact that men moved forward in scientific discoveries because of the Christian presupposition of a Creator God who has given us an ordered universe. In a purely arbitrary universe there wouldn't be the regularity the world reveals. It was because men believed in God that they looked for regularity, in this sense physics is a Christian science. Even here faith has had its function, as it does today in medical science, technological science, and in the social sciences. The fact that some Christians have been bigoted, and idolized their systems of thought until they were out of step with truth, does not rule Christian faith out. Many humanistic scholars, who have their Ph.D.'s in their specialized field, are likewise bigoted and closed to other fields, and remain in kindergarten theologically. Evangelism must enter into dialogue with such in an effort to lead them to honest inquiry into the meaning of life.

Although God as person is to be met and not just reasoned about, the affirmations of the Christian faith remain reasonable. The Christian faith affirms: first, that there is nothing worthy of our supreme devotion short of the reality upon which our lives ultimately rest; second, that in search for the meaning of life one cannot stop short of God; third, that this God is personal; fourth, that all moral obligation finds its final source of "oughtness" in the nature of God; and fifth, that the surest evidence of what God is like is found in Jesus Christ. In support of this the Christian faith affirms that God has unfolded a revelation of Himself in history, that there is a judgment of God to be seen in one's personal life and in the events of history, that God operates in a way consistent with a justice that answers to the entire universe, that man has potential for great possibilities and tragic failures, and that there are evils suffered in this world which are not caused by God.

I. *The Nature of the Knowledge of God in Biblical Revelation*

The Scriptures never seek to present an apologetic or a proof of God's existence. Rather, the Biblical accounts assume faith in God, affirming that God has acted in history. The Biblical account begins with the affirmation that God is Creator, and man was made in God's image, rather than being a super-ape. The Creator God is presented as One who continues to involve Himself in the affairs of the world, rather than, as deism claims, that God started the world on its course, then backed up and let it run on its own. Throughout the scope of Scripture the unifying theme is the redemptive purpose of God who involves Himself in the problems of man, even after man has slapped Him in the face. This involvement is the expression of divine mercy, from the sparing of Noah and his family in the flood-judgment of the world to the personal involvement of Himself at Calvary.

The record of the Bible is not the story of man's search after God, but of God's revelation of Himself. Throughout the Scripture there is an unfolding of this revelation that culminated in Christ. Up until Christ the revelation was in the form of messages and miracles that spoke about God: in Jesus Christ God Himself came to man to make the self-disclosure complete. In the early stages of this self-disclosure in the Old Testament God met a very primitive man where he was, with a revelation that in comparison to the fullness of Christ was primitive in degree. Paul writes that in "the time of this ignorance" God closed His eyes to certain things, but now with the fullness of disclosure in Christ He calls men to thoroughgoing repentance. Through the Old Testament there is a progression toward the New, with sub-Christian levels as seen in polygamy or the attitude of the people of God toward enemies, a progression that led to the coming of Christ—"in him dwelleth all the fulness of the Godhead bodily." Evangelism announces the redemptive activity of God through both Old and New Testaments as interpreted through Christ. The accounts of the Old Testament support the claim of evangelism, that God calls a people to Himself before He outlines an ethic for them.

This revelation came both by person and by proposition. To express it another way, by event and interpretation. Someone has said that Mozart heard his music before he wrote it down, and now people can play it back to us; so the prophets of God heard the voice of God and wrote it down and we can meet God in this Word. The Scripture, the record of God's self-disclosure, is from cover to cover an inspired witness to God as known fully in Christ. This is not a flat-book view of the Scripture, which is then confronted with the problem of explaining differences between the Old and New Testaments as though they were contradictory, but rather sees levels of divine disclosure which by the progress of the unfolding accounts for the differences between the levels. Matt. 5:21. Evanglism is thus an announcement of the redemptive work of God, using any portion of the Scripture, as long as the presentation interprets that Scripture through Christ, who is its Subject and Judge. Luke 24:27.

However, it must be asserted that the disclosure of God culminates in Christ, not only as He is known after the flesh in Jesus of Nazareth, but as known in the risen Lord, and as witnessed to by the Holy Spirit. II Cor. 5:19. This witness, realized fully in the meaning of Pentecost, confirms the teaching of Jesus that God is Spirit, and they who worship Him must worship Him in Spirit and in truth. But just as the knowledge of God in Christ is indissolubly associated with the historic Jesus of Nazareth, so the knowledge of God as Spirit is indissolubly associated with the Word and person of Christ, in whom the reality of the God of Spirit became known to man in concrete form. Evangelism consequently does not assert only that God acted in the ages past, however many thousands of years we may push man's history back, nor only that God acted in Christ from 4 B.C. to A.D. 30, but evangelism asserts that God continues to act in this world in the person of His Spirit. In this sense evangelism is the witness that God is at work redemptively in the world today through the Holy Spirit. John 16:7-14.

II. *The Christian Mind and the Issues of Philosophy*

Earlier it was asserted that theology is philosophy with "a given." This "given" is, of course, revelation. The following comparison of Christian faith and humanism will show its significance for philosophy. In philosophy's search for truth, humanism has reason as its basis, while Christianity adds revelation as the guide for reason. In the object of reflection humanism has nature, while Christianity has first Christ and then nature. The attitude toward history in humanism is cyclical and ontological, while in the Christian faith it is linear and eschatological. As to the norm of ethics, humanism says it is the social good, while Christianity says it is the will of Jehovah. In the attitude toward culture there is a marked difference, for humanism is concerned to create one world, while Christianity affirms that we are strangers and pilgrims here sharing the quality of the eternal kingdom. The philosophy of life is radically different, for humanism is man-centered, while Christianity is Christ-centered. Christian philosophy begins with the "given" of revelation, but it operates by the same philosophical laws of logic and consistency that are generally respected. It also admits its presuppositions and stands in honesty and humble confession that its faith position witnesses to a God who remains the "hidden One" apart from the revelation of Jesus Christ.

Evangelism, to be effective, must be aware of and conversant with the philosophical presuppositions which determine the structure of thought of modern man. Existentialism, which has as its greatest weakness the subjectivism that makes it ultimately humanistic, can be a medium of communication if one capitalizes on a knowledge of ultimate reality that is a "knowledge of" rather than simply a "knowledge about." The famous Thomistic proofs for the existence of God, of first cause, of purpose, of design, of order, and of conception, cannot be used as proofs about God which make faith inevitable. They are rather arguments that make bland unbelief impossible. The avowed atheist must face the fact that he cannot prove that one cannot prove God! Likewise the agnostic or the atheist, either one, must admit that the denial of knowledge of God is a position that cannot be proved by science, and in this sense is a faith position. Evangelism is the task of exposing the false faith of our society, as well as demonstrating that the Christian faith makes more sense out of life than any other position. Acts 17:22-31.

Further, it must be acknowledged that evangelism must take the categories and vocabulary of contemporary thought and pour them full of Christian content. Paul did this with the Greek vocabulary of his day, with words such as grace, lord, and righteousness. Whether Paul Tillich has carried over into contemporary categories the full content of the Christian message is a question aside from the issue here, but he stands as a classic example of a man who has taken the categories and questions of the philosophical world and poured his understanding of the Christian faith into them. The Christian mind, confessing that truth is greater and larger than any man, is not threatened by the variety of categories of thought when it remains clear that truth is ultimately a person and that the revelation of that person transcends at the same time it communicates in the categories of man's reason.

Far too often evangelism has been rendered impotent because the message has been bottled up in either a closed system or in little clichés. Recently on his international broadcast Dr. Billy Graham stated that there are two enemies of evangelism in England today, universalism and an extreme form of Calvinism, evidently meaning by the latter an extreme philosophical determinism. To cope with these problems the Christian church dare not stoop to substituting philosophical arguments for the announcement of the Gospel of Christ; however, it dare not back away from the challenge of exposing the inadequacy and inconsistency of humanism in contrast with New Testament Christianity. First, the heart of universalism is pierced by the cross when it is clear that "God was in Christ reconciling the world unto himself," and the cross is seen as the center of history dividing men on the basis of their attitude toward grace. Second, the problem of determinism is not so easily answered, for the Christian stands with the faith that the program of a sovereign God permeates the whole universe at the same time as God demonstrates the highest form of His sovereignty, within Himself, in the patience and justice which determine His actions and refuses to be threatened even when giving man the freedom to choose treason. These philosophical impasses may serve the proclamation of the Gospel by demonstrating the greatness of the issues that we face even more than if such issues could be reduced to a neat little system.

III. *Evidence in Support of the Christian Faith*

Evangelism is not a theological lecture series in the field of Christian evidences, nor a lecture series in apologetics. Evangelism is rather a declaration, an announcement of the redemptive acts of God in history. Witnessing to the meaning of life under Christ in all its transforming benefits is the greatest contemporary evidence. The claim of the Christian faith that Jesus Christ is risen Lord, that He is contemporary, is the very center of the kerygma. The earliest Christian creed was the brief statement: Christ is Lord. Consequently, transformed lives are a current witness to the reality of Christian faith. Evangelism is thus witness in character, the witness of firsthand relationship with the Lord of the universe, i.e., the Jesus Christ of Nazareth who died for us and rose again. I Cor. 15:14. Hence it may be affirmed that conversions, the transformation of the lives of those that accept the Gospel in sincerity, stand as evidence of the reality of Christian faith. This may be explained as psychological, as purely subjective if looked at only on the surface, but if one inquires deeply enough it stands as evidence of continuity with the message and claims of the Scripture.

In any area of research the intelligent person wants documentary support for his analysis. The documents of the Christian faith stand open before all. In their grand unity they witness to the redemptive acts of God. The uniqueness of the Christ-event is fully attested in the Scripture, including pre-Jesus predictions and post-Jesus attestations. Although contemporary man has not seen Jesus after the flesh, the kerygma announces that this Jesus is Lord and Christ, and as such is the manifestation of the eternal God. Wherever men take His Word by faith and meet Him in prayer they experience the same quality of transformation that is attested in the Biblical accounts of conversions. This continuity of quality is witness to the reality of the contemporary Christ.

There are some things in life for which one does not ask proof; evidence is enough. One may never have seen his paternal grandfather; however, there is no need for proof that he had one. His very life certifies it. We who live today have never seen the Lord of the church, but the church exists, and its very presence certifies the work of its Founder. One may question the validity of the claims of the church, or the claims of the kerygma, but an intelligent person can hardly question the fact that Jesus Christ lived, that He did and said what the records attest.

All of history has been divided by that great central fact of the Christ-event, the meaning of which has altered men's lives, and changed civilizations. Wherever the Christian faith has been taken seriously, civilization has improved rather than retrogressed, and wherever Christian principles have been disregarded, whether among pagans or men who once espoused the Christian faith, that civilization has declined.

From the earliest days of the Christian church the world has been challenged by the superior Christian ethic. Christians confronted Roman culture from the very beginning with a way of peace and love, the building of hospitals, the care of orphans and old people, and their general level of social and moral behavior. The elevation of woman to a new level of equality with man, the challenge to slavery in regarding the lowliest of men as brothers, and the deep concern to sanctify the cultural aspects of life are further evidences of the effect of the Christian faith. Evangelism is the involvement of the Christian church in the problems of humanity in a way that is spiritually creative and socially corrective.

Yet with all of the evidence that might here be compiled, it still remains that the Christ remains the "hidden One" for the natural man. The highest values in human life are personalistic rather than materialistic, demonstrating the necessity of faith for the greatest happiness in interpersonal relationships. By the incarnation the grandeur of divine love is expressed in human forms. Likewise, the quality of the Christian message is emphasized by God's using the medium of faith as the way of saving relationship. Salvation is by grace (the moving of God into our lives in mercy), through faith (the relationship of trust that opens our lives to Him).

It may be argued that the most real realm in the universe is that of mind and spirit. The contemporary mind, concluding that a thing is real only if you can see it, might well be asked the question, "Who has seen mind, or electricity, or pain, or even love?" The realm of the Spirit is real, but is known only through the medium of faith. Evangelism is responsible to show that some things are not proved by standing outside analyzing them, but like love and marriage are known only in the faith experience.

The intellectual challenge of faith is not to discover a system that can force a person by steps of logic to confess Christianity. This is impossible, for persons are not being led to the acceptance of a logical system but to relation with a person. The intellectual challenge of Christian faith is to show contemporary man that life, personality, ultimate reality cannot be reduced to an "it," but that we stand before the Thou apart from whom we could neither think nor exist. The broadening of the mind to confess one's own smallness while conceiving of the greatness of God as known in Christ can lead one to reverence and response.

4

THE THEOLOGY OF
EVANGELISM

*"For I delivered unto you first of all that which I
also received, how that Christ died for our sins according to the scriptures; and that he was buried,
and that he rose again the third day according to the
scriptures." I Corinthians 15:3, 4*

Theology is the statement of Biblical teaching in a systematic
and consistent manner. Evangelism is the communication of that
message with the intent of persuasion. There is the mistaken
opinion on the part of many that theology and evangelism are at
odds. Some hold that evangelism is simply an emotional movement
or a naive presentation of a few simple propositions that call for
a response. Actually evangelism is the proclamation of the evangel,
the kerygma, as an invitation to enter into fellowship with Christ.
Others who claim to major in evangelism hold that theology is dead
and lifeless. They say they are interested only in Christ and not in
doctrine, overlooking the fact that any presentation of Christ as
Saviour and Lord is already a statement of Christian doctrine. It
is imperative that we rediscover that neither theology nor evangelism is complete without the other.

The lack of good theological insight has robbed much of the
evangelistic ministry of the church of content, relevance, and respect. The emphasis on moralism rather than personalism has

2

perverted interpretations of both sin and salvation. Sin is often thought of more in terms of what a person does than why he does what he does. Because of variations in cultural practices sin has been excused with the claim that everything is relative. On the other hand, salvation thought of moralistically has underemphasized relationship with Christ and has failed to respect God's designation that one walking with Christ is a "saint." Col. 1:1, 2. This is due in part to the tendency to equate saints and perfection rather than direction! Again it may be said that instead of a positive announcement of the Gospel there has been negativism, as though the way to cure an ill is to denounce it. There is more to the cure than the diagnosis. It is the remedy that the kerygma proclaims. Rom. 7:12-15.

Obviously an evangelistic witness is not to be a theological lecture any more than music in evangelism should be a classical concert. Both the theological lecture or the concert of classical music presuppose an audience already personally involved in theological or musical appreciation. Evangelism is persuasive proclamation. But no person can witness or preach without in a very few minutes revealing something of his theological presuppositions. The more honest one is about his presuppositions of faith, the more clear his communication and the more readily he is respected.

One need not conclude that to tell the "old story" of the Christ-event is naive, for this is not simply a presentation of a system of thought over against another system, but the introduction of a Person who can step into any system by His transforming presence. Conservative theology is not static. It is dynamic; for although a system of thought may become static, the declaration of a living contemporary Lord is always dynamic by its nature, even though given in the language of a conservative theology that seeks to be true to His self-disclosure. Evangelism dare not apologize for its proclamation, for the evangelist is not presenting a self for which he ought to apologize. The evangelist is presenting the witness of a God who cares.

The question that concerns us in this chapter is, What are the essential aspects of Christian theology that must be out front in the presentation of the Gospel? One should ask himself honestly whether his presentation of the Gospel places Christ out front— makes Him pre-eminent. The Bible presents God as saying, "I am a jealous God . . . and my glory will I not give to another." Of the work of the Holy Spirit, Jesus said, "He shall glorify me: for he shall receive of mine, and shall shew it unto you."

The evangelistic message that is largely a presentation of the deeds and successes of the evangelist is a blasphemous parody rather than a prophetic announcement. God will bless the man with whom He has found His glory is safe! Again a so-called evangelistic message that is primarily a call to social action and obscures the redeeming power of the love and Spirit of Christ is likewise a carnal assertion of man's abilities and a rejection of regenerating grace. Likewise a message that presents the Christian ethic without showing persons how to enter into a Christian experience is only elevating a standard without leading persons to the power of a new life. The theology of evangelism must be the announcement of the essential aspects of life in Christ, of clarifying the meaning, the manner, and the experience of becoming "a new creature."

I. *A Theology of Relationship as the Answer to Man's Estrangement*

When salvation is presented as a saving relationship, a faith relation with a Person, then the gift of salvation is the gift of divine acceptance. The message of the Gospel is that God accepts us in Christ. That is, Christ is our Mediator in the sense of being not only the One who mediates God to us nor only the One who does something on behalf of man before God, but the One in whom both of these dimensions coalesce, the One in whom we enter into a saving relation with God. This gift of God's acceptance can be communicated to a modern world, especially through the general awareness of man's psychological hungers for acceptance, approval, and appreciation. Without cheapening salvation to an "it," as though God gave you something you can run away with and He will never take it back, we can present salvation as relationship, the gift of God's acceptance which He never takes back. This means communicating a God who has opened His heart to us and who will never close us out. The sinner discovers that being lost, that the destruction of hell, is the consequence of closing God out.

The effort at being relevant through communicating a theology of relation is also a guide in interpreting the cross to the modern man. The emphasis on interpersonal relations and the need for harmony between peoples has crystallized the need for forgiveness. Sin is seen at its blackest when thought of as violations of the nature and purpose of personality: as rebellion, as disobedience of the will of God, as irreverence, as an attack upon His person. The problems of moral violations are the expressions of the deeper problem of broken relationships. Disrespect for the person of God always issues in disrespect for persons made in the image of God. Consequently we sin against our fellows by manipulating and using them for our own advantage and pleasure. However, even in sins against our fellows, commonly called crime, or sins against ourselves, commonly called vice, we are guilty of sin against God, called by the Scripture unbelief or disbelief. Deliverance from sin, both sinfulness and sins, comes only by reconciliation with God. Evangelism is the pronouncement that sin is a perversion of the good, while salvation is restoration into fellowship with God and the good. The corrective for sin is not simply denunciation, although sin needs to be exposed as sinful. The corrective is the offer of grace that creates wholeness again.

It may be said here that the preaching of the law must be done carefully, but deliberately. Wesley said, "Before I preach grace I must preach law." The preaching of God's moral standard, whether it be through the Ten Commandments or through the complete standard of the Sermon on the Mount (in which Christ filled full the meaning of the moral law), must be done to expose our sin and not as though in this standard lies our salvation. According to the Apostle Paul, none ever was saved by keeping the law and none ever will be. Rom. 4. Men in the Old Testament were not saved by the law, but by the grace of God. To interpret the Scripture as though men were in one dispensation saved by the law but today are saved by grace is not only untrue to the claims of the Scripture but gives to the listener a difficult view of God. Men were saved in the Old Testament by the grace of God alone, the law exposing their sin but not forgiving it. The sacrifices were the medium of communicating forgiveness as both costly and involving something outside and beyond the transgressor. Moses could only give the law, pointing to man's need of forgiveness, but grace and truth came by Jesus Christ, the God who does the forgiving. Thus effective evangelism uses the law to expose the sin of humanity and presents Christ as the forgiving God.

The message of the cross is set in the context of broken relations between man and God. Man has been guilty of rebellion, of treason, a rebellion exposed by his violation of God's will. Through the Old Testament the prophets verbalized about God, calling man to repentance and mercy. The claim of the New Testament is that in the fullness of time God sent forth His Son—that revelation to be authentic and complete meant that ultimately God Himself would come to man. The Bible says, "To wit, that God was in Christ, reconciling the world unto himself." Confronted with the face of God in Jesus Christ man's rebellion was seen not only as against God's precepts but against His person. In the rejection of Christ man was and is rejecting God.

At the cross man proved his antagonism against the Lord of the universe, seeking to remove God rather than to reverence Him. At Calvary the full intensity of man's sin was expressed, while He "bare our sins [our hostilities] in his own body on the tree." The Bible says, "He . . . should taste death for every man," absorbing the full brunt of man's hostility and speaking back the word of forgiveness. One has said, "He took the sting of man's sin and pulled out the stinger." As William Temple asked, "How can we keep on striking One who takes the blow with such a spirit?" Thus at Calvary, at the same time as man's sin is manifested in all its depth of hostility toward God, divine love is manifested in its forgiving acceptance of man.

One of the relevant ways for evangelism to express the theology of the cross is by the meaning of forgiveness. Forgiveness is hard, the most difficult thing in the world. Especially is it hard if one cares very deeply, for forgiveness means that the one forgiving bears his own wrath against the offense he is forgiving. If one cares deeply about right, about holiness and integrity, his feeling of indignation against the offense is deep. To forgive rather than to take vengeance upon the offender means that the forgiving one, the innocent one, bears his own wrath or indignation rather than to pour it out on the guilty.

In our relation with God we are the guilty ones, the traitors, the disobedient; God is the innocent One whom we have offended, the One who in His holiness feels deeply about sin. Yet He forgives, bearing His own wrath on sin. At Calvary, in His Son, God demonstrated that He suffers the indignities of man and takes them upon Himself, suffering even unto the death, and bears His own wrath, i.e., substitutes Himself in the satisfaction of justice.

Evangelism is the glorious announcement of the grace of God, the forgiving spirit of a God who accepts even a traitor whenever that person is ready to cease his rebellion and come to the God who forgives him. At the same time the cross is a judgment as it exposes man's sin and condemns the man who remains a traitor to such a God. If one will not come to the forgiving God known in the Christ of the cross, "there remaineth no more sacrifice for sins."

II. *Justification as the "Entering into" the Righteousness of Christ*

While the atonement provided by God has just been shown as a move from God's side to achieve at-one-ment with man, the atonement was also an act from man's side, by virtue of Jesus Christ being the One True Man this world has seen. Christian theology seeks to express what happens on man's side as he stands before God in Christ by the term "justification." The word, justification, and the word, righteousness, come from the same Greek word. The unrighteous one is the one not justified before God; the one justified is the one accounted righteous before God or, vice versa, the one counted righteous before God is the one justified. If man's unrighteousness is thought of personalistically, as treason or rebellion rather than primarily moralistically, then his unrighteousness is his estrangement from God or his basic perversity.

Righteousness is then to be thought of as right relation between persons, rather than to be confused with holiness, which is right character in a given person. The question immediately follows: How can a sinner come into right relation with God?

Paul, in answer to this question, says he found it in Christ: "Not having mine own righteousness, which is of the law, but that which is through the faith of Christ, the righteousness which is of God by faith." Evangelism must show the futility of trusting in good works, in religious rites, or in observance of the law to bring one into right relation with God, as though seeking to gain a status by good deed would win God's favor. Man cannot win God's favor by his good deeds while he stands with his back turned on God Himself! Likewise the moralistic thinking that seeks a treasury of merit in the obedience of Christ to be counted in the place of our disobedience, whether this be expressed in terms of the Roman Catholic system or the Protestant system, cannot be the answer.

If righteousness means right relation with God, then such a relation can only be found in Christ. The Bible says, "Of him are ye in Christ Jesus, who of God is made unto us wisdom, and right-eousness, and sanctification, and redemption." And again, "God . . . made him to be sin who knew no sin, so that in him we might become the righteousness of God" (RSV). Thus righteousness is *entered into* in personal relationship, rather than impersonally accounted to us.

In Paul's discussion of this in his letter to the Romans he speaks of Abraham's faith being accounted to him, or imputed to him, for righteousness. Very evidently this is saying that for the righteousness which Abraham did not have God accounted his faith as the satisfying element that certified their relationship. So today, our faith in Christ brings us into a right relationship with God in answer to the problem of our unrighteousness or lack of right rela-tionship with God. Thus when Paul writes to Titus about maintain-ing good works, he is speaking of the works of faith, not works of merit in any effort to gain a treasury of righteousness. Or for a more thorough example, in chapters six and eight of Romans Paul expresses the meaning of having "entered into" the righteousness of Christ—life in the Spirit.

Evangelism is calling persons to come into a right relationship with God in Christ. It is an invitation to discipleship, a sharing His life and His holiness. As will be shown in a later chapter, the Christian ethic grows out of the believer's personal relation with Christ. It is the expression of being a new creature. It finds its norm in the mind of Christ. Evangelism is not only the announcement of God's forgiving grace, but of transforming and enabling grace. As the sixteenth-century reformer, Hans Denck, said, "No one knows Christ truly except he follow Him in life." So evangelism is an invitation to discipleship, a bringing of the whole person under the lordship of Christ.

III. *The New Birth as the Beginning of a New Life in Christ*

Conversion is a redirection of a person's life, a turning from walking away from God to walking with God. The nature of that turn may vary, being for some an immediate about-face, while for others it has been a slow curve, but to be genuine the conversion means a complete redirection. Yet this converted person is the same person going a different direction. He has the same intellect, the same physique, the same emotional make-up—and yet he is different. All of these natural endowments are now under a new power, a new control. Jesus, speaking to a man who had enriched his life by a careful study and practice of religious principles said, "Ye must be born again" (John 3:7). This new birth, of which Jesus spoke to Nicodemus, is confessed repeatedly by such New Testament writers as Paul, John, Peter, and James. It is a descriptive term that expresses what happens to the believer under the creative influence of regenerative grace. The same man is different because of a new life experienced within which in turn makes his behavior different without. Paul says, "If any man be in Christ, he is a new creature: old things are passed away; behold, all things are become new."

The message of the new birth is the answer to man's spiritual deadness, to his loss of spiritual life. This life must be born again. Unregenerate man is incomplete; the top plane of his personality is missing. Man needs a living relationship with God! Man without this vertical dimension is incomplete: he may push out the horizontal dimension to the full, but man made for fellowship with God is incomplete until that fellowship is restored. The birth of spiritual life, the beginning of that fellowship, happens by the operation of divine grace. It is a birth of the spirit by the work of the Holy Spirit. Man must *be* born again; it happens to him, he cannot "born himself." As birth marks the beginning of one's natural life, so the spiritual birth marks the beginning of one's spiritual life. Evangelistic witness leads persons to awareness of their spiritual deadness, and of their need of the life from above. The entrance into this new life is clearly outlined in Jesus' message as through a faith commitment to Himself. Just as marriage marks the beginning of a new life, so fellowship with Christ marks the beginning of a new life in contrast to the old.

The theology of evangelism is the deep central belief that the risen Christ operates today by His Spirit calling men to Himself. When one responds in faith to His convicting call, He seals that believer into fellowship with Himself by the work of the Spirit. Jesus as Lord baptizes with the Holy Spirit those who accept His lordship. The results of this gift of the Spirit are multiple, but the primary one is the spiritual birth which marks the beginning of the spiritual life. Apart from this spiritual birth all practices of religious precepts are merely imitation of the example of Christ, an imitation in which man repeatedly and constantly fails. The spiritual birth is a beginning of fellowship with the Saviour Himself. When this salvation is realized, it becomes clear to the believer that better than getting saved is living with the One who saves you!

The role of theology in evangelism is that of carefulness in putting Christ at the center of every pronouncement, and clarity in elucidating the meaning of life in Christ. The Bible says, "He that hath the Son hath life; and he that hath not the Son of God hath not life." Any emphasis that elevates something else equal to or above Christ is "another gospel," which the Apostle Paul condemned in the Galatians and which stands condemned today. In a modern world, where other gospels are being offered as the answer to man's predicament, the Christian church continues to present the Gospel of Christ. Our age of guilt and escapism will not find its peace apart from the honesty that faces the problem and finds forgiveness in Christ. One has said that the confessional of the modern man is the psychiatrist's couch. This can never suffice, for a man's sin is ultimately against God. Confession of sin is not just the admission of one's faults to another. It is to change one's relation to the Lord. Salvation is far more than acknowledgment of sin; it is a spiritual birth by faith in Christ. Paul said it is "Christ in you, the hope of glory." The Christian is a Christ-indwelled person.

5

THE PLACE OF ETHICS
IN EVANGELISM

*"Therefore to him that knoweth to do good, and
doeth it not, to him it is sin." James 4:17*

Behaving one's beliefs is a continual challenge to every honest
person. Although one can be sincere and be wrong, it is never
wrong to be sincere. The follower of Christ, by the very conviction
that this is life under His lordship, is called to full sincerity. The
Christian ethic is basically a sincere application of the lordship of
Christ to all of life. Rom. 6:1-18. True, one of the greatest moti-
vations for the Christian ethic is gratitude, but this is not its basis.
The Christian ethic is grounded in one's position "in Christ," for
as Paul says, "If any man be in Christ Jesus, he is a new creature."

Our contemporary society needs a new awareness of the Christian ethic. The mass man, the organization man, may be characterized by *anomi, anonymity* and *alienation.*[1] *Anomi* means that
he has no norm for behavior, no absolute, no standard of right and
wrong. The black and white have merged into a gray, and everything is regarded as relative. But the Christian testifies to an absolute, the will of God as known in Jesus Christ. *Anonymity* means

---

1. Waldo Beach, in *Sprunt Lectures,* Union Theological Seminary, Richmond,
1962.

that man has lost his sense of personal identity, of personal worth. Modern man is plagued by the question, "Who am I?" or "Why am I here?" Christians answer: man is God's creation, God's masterpiece, a being created in God's own image for fellowship with Him. *Alienation* means that man because of his broken fellowship with God has broken fellowship with his neighbors. He has lost the ability to be neighborly, is individualistic and selfish, isolated and lonely, frustrated and ever seeking acceptance and approval. The Christian answers by calling man into fellowship with God and by demonstrating Christian community in which each believer relates to his fellow through Christ.

It is true that God was creating a people for Himself before He outlined their ethic of behavior, but this does not mean He is unconcerned about their behavior. After delivering His people from Egypt, creating a people for Himself, He said, "I have redeemed you . . . you are mine" (RSV). Paul in his letter to the Romans, immediately following the great passage on justification by faith, asks a question: Does grace mean that if God freely accepts one into His fellowship, that one can continue to live in sin? His answer is an emphatic negative. To continue in the practices of rebellion is to deny the saving relation of being in Christ. Salvation is deliverance from sin into a dynamic fellowship with Christ. Paul answers, "Sin shall not have dominion over you: for ye are not under the law, but under grace." Rather than being confronted merely by the law which exposes one's sin, the believer has been converted by grace which frees one from sin. Dr. Paul Shearer has said of this passage, "Sin has no power in your life as a believer but what you give it."

Thanks to C. H. Dodd, the Christian church has distinguished between the kerygma (the announcement of the saving news), and the didache (the teachings concerning the will of Christ), thereby emphasizing that the announcement of the good news of salvation in Christ is to be kept in the forefront. However, many have carried the distinction too far, and failed to see that if this salvation is relationship with Christ, the matter of discipleship is inseparable. We need to hear again the question of Amos to those who claim to belong to God but do not walk with Him, "Can two walk together, except they be agreed?" We need to beware of bringing ethics into the center of the proclamation, thereby displacing the person of Christ with moralism, but we must also beware of presenting a mystical Christ who consequently does not change the life of the believer. The modern church must rediscover the authority of Christ, He who is both Lord of the church and Judge of the church.[2] Methods used to renew the church that do not truly renew the church are to be viewed as inadequate.

As a result of the Reformation we have generally interpreted the consequent Protestant movement by four great principles: the supreme authority of the Word of God, justification by faith, the universal priesthood of all believers, and the sanctity of all of life. But it is obvious that the last point has been underemphasized, as well as variously interpreted. In Paul's twelfth chapter to the Romans he presents the Christian life as one of sacrifice, of service, and of sanctity. It is Paul's teaching that the Christian's very body is the temple of the Holy Ghost. This personal relation with God through Christ, which is confirmed by the presence of the Spirit, issues in transformed living. Thus Christian ethics are not appendages to Christian faith, but the very works of faith. This truth has been obscured in the Protestant message by distinguishing between faith and works, rather than between the works of faith and the works of merit. Evangelism does not ignore the Christian ethic; it places it in its proper place, the effect of life in Christ.

I. *Christian Ethics Are Related to Christology in the Same Manner as Salvation Is Related*

Evangelists frequently make remarks about Christian ethic in a way that minimizes the ethic or tends to relate the ethic to salvation (soteriology) as an experience rather than to the lordship of Christ (Christology) as a relationship. Since the Protestant faith has tended to ignore this, there has arisen the problem of antinomianism on one side and legalism on the other. Great evange-

2. A. W. Tozer, "The Waning Authority of Christ in the Church," *Alliance Weekly,* May 1963.

lists have always been men who by the presentation of moral ethics have sought to convince men of their sin and call them to get right with God.

The amazing thing is that so little has been said about the ethic of Christian behavior as the effect of salvation. God is at work making saints out of sinners: He calls us to come walk with Him. We are enjoined to follow holiness, the holiness in which the believer is completely God's possession. This new life in Christ is the evidence that evangelism actually wins people to a new life. The charge that evangelism minimizes the social aspects of the Gospel is not answered, however, by preaching a moralistic system of ethics, but by presenting the personalism of fellowship with Christ which transforms the believer and enables him to be a corrective influence in his social setting.

Should we conclude that the basic attribute of God is His holiness, it appears consistent to say that the most redemptive aspects of that holiness are love and integrity. It follows that if the basic aspect of the Christian ethic corresponds, which is the perfecting of one's character in holiness, the primary evidences are love and integrity. In beginning with God's holiness we immediately move to the exposure of man's sin, emphasizing God's justice. But justice to be consistent with holiness must seek to correct the sinner rather than to destroy him, hence we have God's mercy. The aspect of God's character that keeps the balance between justice and mercy is His sovereignty, the self-control that keeps Him from breaking forth in wrath. Thus God approaches man in love—that which cares deeply, that takes sin seriously yet involves Himself in the problem to correct it. The love principle is not weak; it is dynamic but costly! Evangelism, love for men, compassion, is costly. Col. 1:27.

It may properly be advanced from the New Testament that the central expression of the Christian ethic is love. Jesus said, "By this shall all men know that ye are my disciples, if ye have love one to another." Paul tells us that "the love of God is shed abroad in our hearts by the Holy Ghost which is given unto us." Love means that one's life is intimately open to that of another:

love for God opens one's life to Him and love for one's fellows opens one's life to what God is doing in them. Human nature knows little of love, for love is a totally unselfish giving that delights in the happiness brought to another. Human nature knows much about lust, which is a selfish getting *thing* at the expense of another. Love relates to people, while lust uses people. Evangelism exposes the problems of our selfishness, but also calls us to share the love of God known in Christ, until the very holiness of His presence enables us to both be lovable and to love the unlovely.

Directly associated with the love ethic is that of integrity, of humility, and honesty that orders one's life in a way consistent with the covenant of love entered with Christ. This integrity maintains loyalty or separation unto Christ on the one hand and separation from the anti-Christ spirit and practice of the age on the other. Integrity is the evidence of the sincerity of one's love, of the value placed on the relationship this love provides, and of the purity with which one severs any fidelity to inconsistent relationships. Evangelism is a call to step out and be counted for Christ, to break with the spirit of the age, to declare a new loyalty that is superior to any earthly, social or political loyalties.

This principle calls into question participation in any affairs that are inconsistent with the person who has become Lord in the life of the believer. An imitation of Christ or an attempt to copy the Christian ethic is not what makes a person a Christian; it is fellowship with Christ Himself. But such fellowship in depth cannot conceivably ignore the ethic of the Christ life. Jesus revealed God not only by what He said, but by what He did and what He was. So the Captain of our salvation calls us to accept the mind of Christ as our own, even though it means suffering the tension this creates when it reminds others of their need of life in Christ. The Bible says, "He that hath suffered in the flesh hath ceased from sin; that he should no longer live the rest of his time in the flesh to the lusts of men, but to the will of God" (I Pet. 4:1, 2).

II. *The New Creature Is Expressed by Discipleship in Grace*

Evangelism is essentially the witness-character of discipleship rather than a profession or vocation in which select persons serve. It is the witness that God has involved Himself, and continues to do so, in the lives of men. Redemption is at a cost to the entire Godhead: the Father giving in the Son, the Son giving Himself, and the Holy Spirit giving Himself in His work of calling men to Christ down through the years. The Spirit is God's primary evangelist in the world, and the believers are His tools. He works through men to confront others with the reality of transforming grace. The believer is a disciple *in* grace, not one attempting to earn grace! As one who has experienced grace the believer is a new creature, and the newness of his life—new relationship, new Master, and new motive—all serve to provide evidence that the risen Christ is a reality. Persons who stand outside the faith position of Christianity, who ask for proof of Christ, can be confronted by the living evidence of intelligent men who testify of sharing life with Him, even while they admit that they cannot coerce one into admitting a faith position.

But discipleship is costly. It demands obedience, a humble yieldedness to Christ, a severing of every inferior loyalty. Dr. John Leith has said, "While it is proper for one who is humbly consistent in his attempt to follow Christ to say, 'I'm saved by grace, not by my works,' it is absolutely another thing for a person who is living carelessly to say, 'But I'm saved by grace!' The latter is blasphemy." Evangelism itself is discipleship; it is carrying out the will and witness of the Saviour. The witness must make clear that discipleship is, however, a spirit of life rather than a status. It is not the claim of having reached an ultimate state of maturity. It is rather the confession of a mature decision to live only for Christ.

The lack of concern about Christian ethics has undermined many an evangelistic organization or program. When Christian workers fail to see the meaning of being disciples, they tend to methods and procedures that not only cheapen but pervert the Gospel. Many a man has manipulated people to get himself a following, has used a pet doctrine to label other Christian programs as heresy and thereby "steal their sheep," has used unethical procedures in inviting responses to his preaching of the Gospel, or has operated by questionable and dishonest financial arrangements that has in turn left behind disrespect for the Christian faith. One of the tests of evangelistic work is whether it builds for tomorrow or seeks only a reputation for the present team. Christian activity that is done for the praise of men is always wrong. God blesses the work where His reputation is safe!

III. *Responsible Social Behavior Is Essential to the Kingdom Witness*

The Christian church must always have a redemptive concern for the context in which it has been planted. Human nature is such that we tend to equate morality with the mores of our society, reduce conviction to the conventional, and shrink spirituality to the status quo. Evangelism has always served to sharpen the conscience of society, to call for moral renewal, to confront the world with the fact that all men stand under the ultimate judgment of Christ. Although the church stands on a higher level than the world, within the will of Christ, both stand under His lordship. This is not a dualism of two spheres on a level but two levels of life and loyalty. The fact that the world does not respect Christ does not free them.

The Christian witness to the world is not only witness to a saving experience but to a saving relation, a translation from the level of allegiance to the kingdom "of darkness . . . into the kingdom of his dear Son." The Christian, although a stranger and pilgrim in this world, is always seeking the best, the highest values. Knowing that sin is a perversion of the good, it is the Christian who resists sin and calls the society in which he lives to a higher standard. Thus the kingdom witness involves responsible social behavior.

Ethics have a place in evangelism in this sense as well, for the call to kingdom membership is at the same time an exposure of the perversions of earthly societies. As the first book of the Bible reveals man's attempt to find security in an earthly civilization, so the last book of the Bible shows the crumbling of these civilizations and the eternal nature of the heavenly kingdom. Due to man's idolizing of earthly security at the Tower of Babel God confused the tongues and scattered the people. Gen. 11. But at the very beginning of the church at Pentecost, the gathering of the people of God was certified by the presentation of the Gospel in multiple tongues. Acts 2.

The witness of the disciple is a declaration that he follows another Lord than the lords of this world. Paul refers to the Christian as an ambassador for Christ, a citizen of heaven living in this world who represents his Sovereign and remains true to his homeland. Our world, which seeks its security here, has had to learn by numerous ways that God made this old world to be precarious as a reminder that "here we have no continuing city." Through the church, God is at work taking "out of . . . [the world] a people for his name."

The church, to do its job and to represent its Lord in an intelligible way, must be relevant to its times. If the church only speaks in language understood by itself about the problems within itself to the people it has educated within itself; it doesn't have the right to claim to be involved in the work of the kingdom of Christ, in discipleship, or in fulfillment of the Great Commission. If it only speaks in the clichés of yesteryear and remains withdrawn from the issues of its day, it has ceased to be the salt of the earth. The church has an ethical responsibility to be true to its essential nature, to witness to the grace of God that creates it.

One might speak of this as the risk of evangelism, for in exposing the sub-Christian level of human behavior, evangelism creates tension in a given society. When we truly understand Christ, in His fullness and most profound dimensions, we are presenting One who calls into judgment all of man's carnal behavior. The Christian worker needs to beware of seeking to reduce the Gospel to something that is acceptable to one who remains in sin. You can never popularize Christ!

Repeatedly the Gospel of John tells us, "There was a division among the people because of him." True witness is a communication of the redemptive love of God toward His enemies, but such a witness is always in danger of stirring up the tension that God's enemies express in their rejection of Him. Thus Jesus warns His disciples that the world will hate them, saying in His prayer to the Father, "I have given them thy word; and the world hath hated them, because they are not of the world, even as I am not of the world."

Ethics in evangelism is the constant witness against the perversion of the good which is the essence of man's sin. It is the call to a life of discipleship, of obedience to the will of God. It creates a spirit of life rather than a status, a spirit that seeks to do the will of God in each situation. The evangelist is responsible to demonstrate the Christian ethic in his own ministry, if he would require the Christian ethic of those to whom he ministers.

6

THE CONTRIBUTION OF
EVANGELISM TO CULTURE

*"By him to reconcile all things unto himself;
by him, I say, whether they be things in earth,
or things in heaven." Colossians 1:20*

When we think of culture we think of quality, of refinement, of taste, of class. There is nothing "cheap" about Christianity, for Christianity is the correction of man's perversions and the calling of man to the best—life in Christ. The highest values are found within the Christian faith, the values of personality and of principle, of love and forgiveness, of peace and harmony, of truth and loyalty, of purity and nobility of character. An honest look at Jesus Christ reveals that He was the most dignified Man the world has ever seen. In fact, the Bible teaches that since man's fall in sin the whole of human life is depraved, and we only discover what man was intended to be like when we look at Jesus Christ. He was the only "true Man" the world has ever seen.

As the only genuine Man the world has ever seen, the Son of Man taught and demonstrated the qualities of life that have enriched every culture where Christianity has been truly presented. Wherever Christianity has been subsumed under humanistic purposes or philosophy, with man acting as lord and Christ being used as man's tool, things done under the name of Christian faith have perverted the Gospel and hindered evangelism to this day. The Moslems still equate Christianity with the Crusades, the Hindus remember that Gandhi was told to leave a Christian church because he was not a European, or the communists point to the Inquisition as evidence of the intolerance of Christians when they claim that Christianity has no better record than atheism. Granting that they can build a case against the church, because of the many compromises the church has made of the true essence and character of Christian faith, a strong case can be built for Christianity. We must study honestly what the Christian faith has done in various cultural settings where its presentation has been consistent with its vital essence.

Before discussing the nature of the contribution of evangelism to culture, it is important to review the characteristics of culture itself. In the first place, culture is ubiquitous. It is everywhere present; every person is a part of a particular type of culture. America, by its historic sociological make-up is an amalgamation of various cultures. However, through the years there has developed a particular type of American culture that permeates the whole.

In the second place, culture is varied, as seen in the previous affirmation that America is a cultural amalgamate, in which the whole is made up of the varied patterns. This is often the cause of divisions in churches, and in a large way accounts for the choices of many people as to which denomination offers them a more desirable program. Evangelism in America is confronted with real difficulties in a class structure that is as rigid in many ways as the caste system in the Far East.

Third, culture is continually changing. It is in a state of flux, as is obvious in the transition from the horse and buggy to the realms of supersonic jets and space travel, or from the pumpkin ball to the hydrogen bomb, or from the pony express to the contemporary Telstar communication. Even the distinctions of thought which characterize difference between rural and city culture are fast being erased through the medium of television, which educates the rural mind in the same fields as the city mind.

In the fourth place, culture in itself is neutral, not evil, even though it is tempted to idolatry. Christianity supersedes man's culture, and can permeate any particular one with the meaning of "heavenly citizenship."

In the fifth place, culture is pliable; it can be shaped by various influences. This means that the Christian, as "the salt of the earth," has a redemptive influence within culture that adds to its quality. Evangelism contributes to a given culture as "the light of the world."

Sixth, culture is the scene of conflict, the stage in which the divine and the demonic are revealing before the gaze of the universe and of man which one has the superior quality. It is on the stage of culture, rooted in the very fiber of history, that God is working out His redemptive purpose.

Finally, culture is perishable. This is not the eternal state, and no culture will exist forever. Some cultures, like that of Rome, have gone out like a light. For those who find their security in a given civilization or culture, evangelism is a reminder that "the world passeth away, and the lust thereof: but he that doeth the will of God abideth for ever" (I John 2:17).

I. *The Higher Loyalty Is Our Directive in Cultural Involvement*

Just as there are two levels in Christian experience, the immature level of legalism, and the higher level of freedom in Christ, so there are two levels of human position under the lordship of Christ: the lower level of the world that does not live by (but will be judged by) that lordship, and the higher level where the church lives in the perfection of Christ. The directive of the Christian in culture comes from the highest level, his position in Christ. The separation of church and state must be thought of in this same manner, both standing under the lordship of Christ, with the state on the lower level that refuses to recognize His lordship and the church on the higher level that is to live by His lordship. In Romans in the thirteenth chapter, where Paul writes of the Christian's place in the state, the state is clearly seen as a secondary authority that stands under the primary authority of God by which the state is ordained. In any culture evangelism must witness to man's call to the highest allegiance, reminding men that in declaration of loyalties "we ought to obey God rather than men."

Paul speaks of the church as a colony of heaven on earth. This heavenly citizenship, this higher loyalty, this supreme ethic, is the directive for the Christian. We are elevated to "sit together [with him] in heavenly places," a position that calls us to a redemptive ministry in the world. Wherever the church has sought to control society, it has made improper alliances. The search to be in charge is wrong. Christ called us not to be lords but to be servants, to express the deepest values of life by an emphasis on personhood that would serve rather than manipulate. Jesus said, "My kingdom is not of this world: if my kingdom were of this world, then would my servants fight." In contrast, He sends His followers out as sheep in the midst of wolves, as meek as sheep who can do nothing but witness of their presence. We are sent as witnesses, commissioned to carry the Gospel into all the world. Evangelism contributes to any given culture by challenging persons to the highest values, to life in God, to an awareness of their responsibility before ultimate truth as Person, to an understanding of man's dignity in the image of God, and to an awareness of principles which enable one to be neighborly.

True Christianity is creative; it is not static or passive. A survey of various cultures soon makes it evident that the contribution of special revelation has been a tremendously enriching power. Having transformed our concept of history from a repetitious spinning of the wheels to a concept of divine purpose which views it as linear, it speaks to the aspects of purpose and values which Christian faith creates in the life of a simple individual. The creative benefits of Christianity may be surveyed in the whole of human values. The Christian view of personality itself is creative, a testimony to the dignity of man over animal. The multiple programs of social concern and service, for the orphans and the aged, the poor and the ill, the blind and retarded are only a few witnesses to the impact of evangelism in our culture. The American home, standing in a precarious position today, being threatened with internal breakdown by the moral laxity of our time, is an illustration of what happens culturally when Christian principles are rejected. The only cure for this ill is the evangel of Christ, calling men and women back to the principles which make lifelong commitment and sanctified sharing a reality. The Christian church has the potential of enriching and elevating the culture in which it is planted if it will communicate the values of being in Christ.

II. *The Mission of the Church in Culture Is Witness in Character*

The Christian church does not close itself to the contributions of technical, empirical, or normative sciences. Rather, it is enriched by them at the same time as it enriches them by the content of revelation. Neither does the church dare take the dogmatic position that the only place one finds truth is within the church, for humanness of believers means that we are limited in perception even while we have declared our loyalty. On the other hand, the Christian church dare not sell out to culture, as though the conventional needs no correction or as though verbalization of faith in Christ becomes a sacrament that counterbalances the unrighteousness of the status quo.

Evangelism is many times an exposure of the ills of society, a diagnosis of the illness of man, a judgment of God applied here and now as men are made aware that they stand today under the ultimate judgment of Christ. This judgment must not be thought of simply as future, for each act today stands not simply under the judgment of friends or society but ultimately under the judgment of Christ. One of the most serious things about human existence is that one will always be the kind of person that has done what he has done today! The marvel of His grace is that God forgives so completely that, while we as forgiven sinners are in heaven because of His grace, each reminder of the cost God paid on Calvary will not induce Him to throw our sins up to us again—it is finished.

A Christian ethic that claims a superior loyalty and applies it at a cost of separation has often been referred to as withdrawal. Obviously if such an ethic is applied in evangelism, calling our society to the higher loyalty of Christ even at the cost of suffering their hostility, this cannot be regarded as withdrawal. The separated life of the Christian, when it is consistent in its spirit and structure of behavior, serves its culture by purifying it. As members of the spiritual kingdom, we serve our culture in a way consistent with the essential nature of our profession.

First, the Christian serves society by exposing its unbelief and calling it to Christ. Second, we serve our society by challenging it to a higher level of moral integrity. Third, we contribute to our culture by maintaining our personal integrity when others about us are selling out. Fourth, we serve our culture by demonstrating discipleship in a materialistic society, living for the values of personality rather than material. Fifth, the Christian church serves its society by building basic social institutions, such as families, churches, schools, and hospitals. Sixth, the Christian serves society by rejecting violence and demonstrating the way of redemptive love. And finally, the Christian serves society by calling men to heavenly citizenship.

Such a contribution to culture is evidently not withdrawal, but it is a quality of service that means deep personal involvement. Evangelism in depth speaks to the whole of life. We properly speak of saving souls, but not meaning a little entity within man; we view the man himself as a living soul. The convert's whole life is to be transformed by the lordship of Christ and the presence of His Spirit.

III. *The Creativity of Evangelism in the Conscience of Society*

Many persons have no sense of their need of a Saviour because they do not sense their being lost. Evangelism must create an awareness of man's responsibility before the Sovereign of the universe, an awareness of man's estrangement and perversions, and an awareness of the destruction that sin brings now and the eternal separation of hell. In a society which uses God's name in vain, and jests about heaven and hell as if they were merely fables from the fairy stories of childhood, there is the need for a new conscience on sin. A society that has lost its norm, its sense of an absolute, its reverence before God, needs a prophet of righteousness. As the prophet Amos, who has well been called "God's angry man," so evangelism must run the risk of being labeled at times as negative. But being negative at points is not negativism, for just as a physician must diagnose the case and even administer surgery that the healing may result, so a prophet of God must at times expose the ills of society in a painful analysis, in order that the corrective of spiritual healing may follow.

As a current illustration, it would be impossible to evaluate the contribution being made to American culture by Billy Graham, in his Amos-like message to a nation plagued by moral decay. No one can measure how much his messages in crusades, on radio and television, and in the printed page have done as a corrective in problems of divorce and delinquency, as well as in producing a conscience on many other things. One can only say, "Thank God that our generation has seen God work through Dr. Graham throughout the world." But what is illustrated in this man of prominence is just as true in quality if not as great in quantity through the lives of thousands of relatively unknown Christians whose consistent testimony serves to enrich their personal worlds.

We need to remind ourselves that God will not clean up the world by our majority vote. Our contribution to society is not an attempt to bring in a "golden age." God is working in the theater of historic cultures in a manner that works out His divine purpose. He is taking out of the world a people for His name. Cultures roll on while God in sovereign patience restrains wrath and expresses mercy to win more persons to Himself. To have made man without the potential of talking back to Him would have been less than God's purpose in making man on a level capable of fellowship with Himself. To coerce man would be to violate man's essential nature as a being in the image of God. Consequently, God's redemptive work is carried on in a way consistent with His holiness, in which love and justice both find satisfaction. Evangelism is the witness of the Gospel by which God's redemptive work is carried forward, penetrating the realms of the demonic at the same time as it remains true to the principles of the divine program.

7

THE MISSION OF THE
LOCAL CONGREGATION

*"That the name of our Lord Jesus Christ may be
glorified in you, and ye in him, according to the grace of
our God and the Lord Jesus Christ." II Thessalonians 1:12*

The local congregation is God's primary means of evangelizing a given community. The true church is a "habitation of God through the Spirit." It is composed of redeemed sinners who have experienced a spiritual birth and share fellowship in the Spirit. Eph. 2:22. This fellowship is first with God through Christ, and second with one's brother in Christ. Christian community is a creation of faith; it is the result of relating to one's brother through Christ. Consequently, where true "church" happens, the believers relating to one another through Christ, this worshiping community is evangelistic, for the same believers will relate to their neighbors through Christ. Evangelism is the witness of the Spirit through a believer whose firsthand relation with Christ speaks to those outside of Christ.

In the New Testament period the local churches were nerve centers of evangelism. The church is really the church when the worshiping community expresses the depth of its worship or devotion to Christ by witnessing of Him to others. Worship is not simply a ritualistic confession, but it is a redemptive communication. If the worshiping community truly worships, it will do this in a greater manner than just in the eleven o'clock service on Sunday morning. Much of the language in contemporary discussions of the nature of the church revolves around the concept of the corporate nature of the church.

The rediscovery of koinonia, of the sharing brotherhood, is essential to rediscovering the true nature of fellowship. But the church is first of all an ecclesia, a body of persons who have been called by God's Spirit to partake of His grace. This calling into the body of Christ is personal and individual; it may be mediated through the koinonia in a corporate context or by an invitation into fellowship by some lone personal evangelist. But in the moment the witness leads the converting soul in communion with Christ, the Saviour is present—church happens!

Obviously one isn't born into a family and then regarded as an orphan, nor is one brought to Christ to live apart from His brethren. One who is joined to the Head of the church in full commitment will find his rightful place in the body. I Cor. 12:12. The convert becomes a disciple, one who takes his place in the community of believers, bearing his cross before the world among whom he once stood in rejection of *the cross*. This witness identifies him with the gathered believers, among whom he now shares the spirit of the new life. Within the gathered community he in turn finds that the gifts of the Spirit which are his in grace enable him to be a contributing partner and not a parasite. If that gathered community is truly the church, it will both recognize those gifts for internal sharing and permit the Spirit to broaden the church's outreach and views by respecting as a brother one whose conversion opens new areas of penetration into the world.

In much of contemporary theology the nature of the church as a community of believers has enlarged the former understanding of the church as a means of grace. The emphasis is more correctly now being placed on what Elton Trueblood calls *The Company of the Committed*. The danger is that this healthy emphasis is often turned into an interpretation of the redemptive community that is next thing to idolatry. The modern church may be concentrating more attention and devotion upon the structure of the church than upon the Saviour Himself. Although the church is the witness of Christ in the world, the conscience to society, the fellowship of forgiven sinners, it is only Christ who is Redeemer, the Head of the church, and the Saviour of the world. One truly shares in the church as he shares in Christ. Matt. 16:18. Correspondingly it is when one truly shares in Christ that he in turn shares Christ with others. It is in this manner that any church, any congregation, becomes evangelistic, sharing Christ with those who do not know Him. This experience of grace which is in turn expressed in witness is the evangelistic spirit of the church. II Cor. 5:20.

It is in the local congregation that the church is truly visible. Here believers gather to worship and depart to witness. Here believers testify to one another of their personal joy in Christ and find encouragement to testify to unbelievers of their need of Christ. The atmosphere of the worship hour must carry an evangelistic tone if it is truly Christian, for Christian worship is always a response to God's grace that calls us into His fellowship. Where the presentation of the Gospel carries only the tone of ethical admonitions, it is inconsistent with the kerygma, for the Gospel is essentially personal and relational. When the worshiping body is truly responding to divine grace, it is a witness to sinners present as to how they may appropriate grace. It follows that the pastor is thus conditioning his flock to penetrate society with the witness of Christ.

I. *Redemptive Involvement in Society—a Strategy of Penetration*

In his philosophy of missions, Dr. Donald A. McGavran has pointed out that just as electric current flows best where there is good contact, so with the Gospel. We need more saints in shoe leather, persons who behave their beliefs, persons who deliberately get themselves involved in contact with others for purposes of witness. The Christian is the "salt of the earth," and to make its contribution salt must lose itself in that to which it contributes. However, "if the salt have lost his savour," its power of ministering is gone. So the Christian is saved out of the world in the deliverance from slavery to the spirit of the age, thereby preserving the saving qualities, to in turn be sent again into the world to a ministry that affects others redemptively. It is at the level of the local congregation that the contact is most effectively made with the world. Here is the front line in the battle with the realm of darkness.

Focusing on the pastor, this means that his mission is the edifying of the people for the work of the ministry. See Eph. 4:12. Ministering to the world about us is not confined to the role of the pastor. In fact, it may be said that the pastor is God's gift to the church; the church is God's gift to the world! The pastor should be building mature Christians with the goal before him of multiplying witnesses in the world. It is his responsibility to create a sense of mission among his flock, to inspire them in hours of worship to be their best for Christ in daily witness. As a great man is one who can find greater men and put them to work, so a good pastor is one who makes ministers out of others. Let the pastor clarify his vision, reaffirm his goal, and outline his strategy to achieve this goal and things will begin to happen. There is a simple law that following certain principles results in a particular end. We get the results which our principles of operation predetermine. When the life of a congregation is lived from committee room to committee room, we can expect the deadness of an ingrown social clique. If the life of a congregation is lived from worship to witness, even the committees where groups meet to "weigh" the issues will be transformed with depth involvement.

Focusing on the personal witness who scatters into society to live Christ before men, attention must be given to the matter of communication. Among other things, communication depends upon mutual interest and mutual understanding. For example, kindred vocational interests and understanding make it easier for persons to understand one another when they verbalize their faith. Strategy of penetration calls for an awareness on the part of the congregation that as each moves in his particular world, both geographical and vocational, they will meet many persons with whom they already have a point of contact. The preconditioning factors, such as reputation and relevance, determine much of the success of one's witness. This means that the potential for evangelism in a given congregation is much greater in the laity than in the clergy. The pastor who works creatively does not simply run a counseling program for personality conflicts within a group that continually reviews one another's idiosyncracies. He turns the attention of his people to Christ and His compassion and sends them out with the healing balm of a mission of sharing. What witness is there who has not found that in going to another in a service of faith he himself has been enriched?

Focusing yet upon the persons witnessed to, it may be said that human nature is everywhere basically the same—people want to be treated as persons, not as objects! God doesn't give up cases because of the hard-shell bluff; neither should we. Psychology teaches us that every person wants to be accepted, approved, and appreciated. The quest for this satisfaction dominates man's behavior. Many fail to even think deeply about the group in which they seek this status and disregard its quality, if only they feel accepted and appreciated.

The peer-group idol betrays many a seeking soul. The significant thing, however, is that this pursuit reminds us that the satisfaction sought is not in the group but in the inner sense of having these hungers satisfied. The Christian witness recognizes this, and points to a satisfaction of quality through the grace of God. Here the lost and lonely soul can find complete acceptance, the security of being approved in Christ, and the assurance that God appreciates the return to fellowship. Strategy of penetration involves the witness in depth understanding of the inner drives that determine behavior, making the presentation of the Gospel truly relevant. We need to be reminded that people will still come to the Saviour and to His church when they discover that they are wanted.

II. *Assimilating New Believers—a Test of Spiritual Maturity*

The evidence of our faith that the Gospel has the power to change the life of another is seen in our willingness to accept a forgiven sinner. We have not really risen above self-righteousness until we can accept another sinner into the brotherhood of the redeemed as equal. As long as we feel threatened by assimilating new personalities, we are betraying our own insecurities. Spiritual maturity involves complete satisfaction in our commitments as well as mature comprehension. Such maturity is not threatened by the immaturity of new converts and their ideas, but accepts such as the call to mutual sharing and spiritual ministry.

Too often we fail to take the positive approach of sharing in the development of a disciplined and mature brotherhood. It is not difficult to find the pessimist, the critic, who can predict the decline of the congregation when it assimilates new converts and immature minds into its fellowship. How much higher the calling of using the spiritual gifts which the Spirit gives to the congregation through its various members as ministries to the brotherhood. Through such involvement the immature are caught up in a spiritual fellowship.

Church is a continuous creation of the Spirit. It is not something static, and by its very nature every member is creating the particular expression of "church" a given community is receiving. Maintaining a disciplined congregation, separated from the world, is not done by setting some level of life as a static level to defend but by the dynamic of sharing in the obedience of the Spirit that calls all to the authority of the Word.

New believers must have a sense of being wanted, not in an expression of sugar-coated condescending love, but in a true awareness that they are among brethren, redeemed sinners with whom they have this essential characteristic in common. When any church group becomes sociologically centered in certain cultural characteristics as their rallying point, it becomes well nigh impossible for persons with a vastly different culture to become wholly involved at this point.

It is the nature of the church that the spiritual relation with Christ as redeemed sinners is central rather than some lesser element. This does not mean a reaction against a particular culture, for every person has certain cultural structures in which he expresses his understanding of life. What it does mean is a refusal to idolize that culture and prove the same by placing it second. Only the spiritual relationship is so evidently predominant that the spirit of fellowship supersedes the social differences. The church is not really the church until it can express its true nature by extending the full expression of brotherhood to persons who are ever-so-recent in their commitment to Christ.

Evangelism is thus one of the tests as to whether a worshiping group is more than a mutual admiration society, an organization for devotional therapeutics, an opportunity for development of aesthetic appreciation, or a weekly class in Christian ethics. As fire exists by burning, so the church is said to exist by evangelism. The gathered community expresses the degree in which it is committed to the communication of the Gospel by its attitude toward the world outside its borders. A church that can let the world go its way and the congregation another is not truly His church. The church which Christ planted in a hostile world, the church purchased by His own blood, is a church on the offensive that moves into enemy territory to win persons to Christ. It is His body, functioning to perform the functions which the Head of that body seeks to perform in the world. Those functions must be consistent with the cross, with the redemptive love that characterized the whole mission of Christ. There is a real sense in which the church is a continuation of the work of the cross, the body which by its witness of fidelity to Christ continues to both create and absorb hostility from the world.

III. *The Priority of "Presence" in the Worship Program*

To speak of spirit in a meeting or assembly is to refer to something intangible; to speak of program is more concrete. What the Christian church needs today is the sense of "presence" more than satisfaction with its program. Often persons refer to meetings with terms like "warm," "meaningful," or "spiritual," by which terms they mean something more wholistic than simple intellectual involvement. Worship is not simply a meeting with academic characteristics. It is the reverence of faith before the risen Christ, whose "presence" is communicated by the Holy Spirit. Simply running through the ritual of a program does not guarantee that the congregation is experiencing this "presence." True koinonia can only be experienced when there is the common experience of sharing in Christ. It is the "presence" of God among His worshiping people that convicts the sinner of his loneliness and estrangement from God. The local congregation must prayerfully seek this awareness of "presence" in its gatherings if it would truly express the nature of the church to visitors who come to discover its life. I Cor. 14:24, 25.

One of the dangers inherent in this emphasis is that persons will interpret freedom of emotional expression as though this is synonymous with "presence." Such freedom and involvement accompanies true koinonia, but the essential characteristic of fellowship is more than emotional liberties. I Cor. 14:29-33. There are various conditioning factors which become avenues by which God communicates Himself to us. While a rather formal recitation of the Apostles' Creed may be used of the Spirit to communicate "presence" to some, for another it may be in the extemporaneous testimony of a believer. Likewise, there are some persons whose preconditioning experiences can find them involved in worship in one type of music, while another may have more openness to the sense of "presence" through other music. The common element is wholistic involvement, in which true believers unite in affirming with the warmth of true devotion that Christ is the very center of their lives.

The sense of "presence" is not to be limited to the eleven o'clock service on Sunday morning. All of life is to be a sacrament. The believer presents his very body as a living sacrifice, as the temple of the Holy Ghost. I Cor. 6:19. There are no realms of life which are not to be permeated by the awareness that God through the Spirit is mediating a sanctifying influence there. The sense of presence in the gathered community is not something which happens there automatically but is the result of what each believer brings with him to the corporate fellowship. I Cor. 12:24-27. Conversely, the sense of "presence," which the individual carries with him through the week, is strengthened by the mutual sharing in the corporate body. The local congregation is the gathering where as believers we strengthen one another's hand in the Lord, contribute to one another in interpretations of the faith, and support one another in the awareness that we share a dynamic fellowship. The believer carries this sense of "presence" into the secular world, and by doing so is a witness who points others to spiritual reality. II Cor. 4:1-7.

The next chapter will deal with the role of the Spirit in evangelism, but this role is not to be thought of apart from the sanctifying work of the Spirit in the lives of believers whereby He creates witnesses and extends the true nature of the kingdom. The Christian refuses to separate belief from action, and by behaving his beliefs he expresses the meaning of transforming grace. One who is truly Christian is a Christ-indwelled person. He does not live his life alone, for coupled with his sense of belonging in the local congregation is the sense of "presence" that inspires him.

The congregation is the primary channel of evangelism in a community. Its program must be consistent with the essential nature of "the church." It is not simply "a" church in isolation, but a functioning part of the body of Christ. Just so, missions and evangelism are not programs which bypass the church, but which express the essential life of that church. D. T. Niles has said, "A mission that is distinct from the church is like a 'floating kidney' it must be anchored some place." We are laborers *together* with Him.

8

THE PRIMACY OF THE
SPIRIT'S ROLE

*"And my speech and my preaching was not with enticing
words of man's wisdom, but in demonstration of the Spirit and
of power: that your faith should not stand in the wisdom
of men, but in the power of God." I Corinthians 2:4, 5*

As one cannot think of the Gospel without thinking of the
work of Christ, so one cannot think of evangelism without thinking
of the work and witness of the Spirit. Acts 1:8. Evangelism is
more than simply giving a theological lecture on Christian evidences. It is a witness of a genuine Christian experience. Truth
is a living power, it is personal, and divine truth has an inner
dynamic because it is mediated by the presence of the Spirit. When
we think of the Spirit we think of presence, of perception, and of
potency. The power is not that of mere physical force, but the
inner dynamic of spiritual reality. In the proclamation of the
Gospel we may argue ever so carefully and consistently, but one
is not converted from sinfulness just by being convinced that he is a
sinner. There must be the inner conviction and call of the Holy
Spirit. Jesus said that no one could come to Him "except the
Father . . . draw him." It is this convicting and calling power that
is our concern in this chapter.

Recognizing from the Apostle Paul's writings that the church
is a creation of the Spirit (Eph. 2:22), it must be affirmed that the

twentieth-century church must rediscover the presence and role of the Spirit. To be true to its essential nature the church cannot be satisfied with program, or organization alone. The church is a fellowship of forgiven sinners in whose midst the living Christ is present *by His Spirit*. It is the Spirit who calls men to Christ, who quickens them to spiritual life, who unites them in confession of Him as Lord, who enriches the brotherhood by the multiple gifts He endows, who sanctifies the lives of those who are in Christ, and who uses them as tools in His work of evangelism. The Christian church must be Christ-centered for perfection, Bible-centered for permanence, and Spirit-centered for power. This triune center is the total involvement of the divine in the church, the human expression of the body of Christ.

Evangelism is a primary role of the Spirit in the world. John 3:3-5. The Holy Spirit is God's Evangelist, calling men and women to Christ. He uses men and tools, but it is the Spirit who calls the sinner to the Saviour. Thus the attitude of any congregation toward evangelism is indicative of their relation to the Holy Spirit. Any congregation or church that fails to be evangelistic is not simply differing with methods of work or kinds of program, but is failing the Holy Spirit and is inconsistent with His will. The Spirit endows the church with gifts in ways that perpetuate its vitality, its vision, and its victory. Heb. 2:4. When a church fails to exercise those gifts through a lack of obedience, that church suffers by the shrinkage or wasting of inactivity. All efforts to produce a semblance of koinonia by programing will fail, for true koinonia is a creation of the Spirit and occurs in proportion to our conformity to His will.

I. *The Spirit as "Lord of the Harvest"—God's Evangelist*

One of the titles given to the Holy Spirit is "Lord of the Harvest." Jesus told His disciples to pray the Lord of the Harvest to send forth laborers into the harvest. Later He announced that it was necessary for Him to return to glory that the Holy Spirit might come as the divine Personality continuing the redemptive work in the world. The disciples were instructed about His work and told to tarry in Jerusalem until they received "the power of the Holy

Ghost" coming upon them. The entire Book of Acts is a presentation of all that Jesus continued to do through the Spirit. Acts 1:1, 2. The believers are the lips through which the Spirit speaks to the world, the arms by which He reaches out in compassion, and the lives through which He demonstrates the transforming grace of Christ.

The Holy Spirit is extending the kingdom of Christ throughout the world. Jesus said, "And when he is come, he will reprove the world of sin, and of righteousness, and of judgment." Following the statement He interpreted it, explaining how the Spirit does this work. The Spirit convinces the world of sin—"because they believe not on me"—by glorifying Christ in the lives of believers. He convinces the world of righteousness—"because I go to my Father, and ye see me no more"—by reminding the world through the believers' lives that righteousness (right relation with God) is a possibility. He convinces the world of judgment (now! not judgment to come)—"because the prince of this world *is* judged"—by demonstrating through the lives of believers that sin is both condemned and overcome in the life of faith. This is to say that the effectiveness of the Spirit's communication is conditioned by the character of the church or lives of the believers. John 16:7-14.

Here again we are face to face with the imperative of a high ethical standard among the people of God. Not only is the church a habitation of God through the Spirit, but individual lives are the temple of the Holy Ghost. God calls us to follow holiness, to discover all that it means to belong completely to Him. Heb. 12:14. Confessing Christ as Lord we are confessing that we are His subjects. Being translated from the kingdom of darkness into the kingdom of Christ, we live by another standard. God calls His own to lives separated unto Him, lives that share the victory of the Spirit over the carnality of the self, lives that are nonconformed to what they once were by being conformed to Christ. II Cor. 6:17-20. Victory over the world within us as well as the world about us is realized by living on a higher plane, living "in Christ" rather than in the flesh.

II. *The Spirit as Creator of Witnesses—Communicating Christ*

Through the church the Spirit convinces the world of its need of Christ; within the church the Spirit glorifies Christ. Jesus said, "He shall glorify me: for he . . . shall take of mine, and shall shew it unto you." A witness is one who speaks out of personal knowledge of a matter. To be a witness of Christ one must have a personal knowledge of Him. Phil. 3:10-12. This is not merely a knowledge about but a knowledge of Christ. Existentialist thought has called this distinction to our attention today. As one may readily see the difference between a knowledge about marriage and a knowledge of marriage, so the difference is clear between a knowledge about and a knowledge of Christ. The Spirit communicates Christ to the believer, and by his experience with the risen Christ the believer is made a witness. The Spirit's work of evangelism is mediating Christ to believers that they become eye witnesses of His glory!

Too many persons are guilty of spiritual plagiarism; they have taken the moral teachings of Christ and rejected His person. One is not a witness who only lectures on ethical teachings; one is a witness when he communicates the reality of spiritual experience, of relationship with Christ. The new birth, Spiritual birth, is an absolute necessity for salvation and for witness. No person can truly witness of Christ unless he has been born of the Spirit, unless he is in Christ.

Christian experience is not simply an imitation of the life of Jesus; it is identification with Jesus Christ. Gal. 2:20. Paul says, "Henceforth know we no man after the flesh: yea, though we have known Christ after the flesh, yet now henceforth know we him no more." To evangelize is not to create a hero worship of Jesus as a "Lincoln" of some past century. Evangelism is to call people to a spiritual experience, a spiritual birth, a new life that begins the moment one opens the center of his life to Christ the Lord.

But the Holy Spirit is a person, not simply an experience, not an *it*. The new birth is the entrance upon a new life. It is an about-face from the old life of going our own way; it is the reorientation of the heart or center of one's motivation. Eph. 2:8-10. The grace of God not only offers forgiveness, a release from guilt; it offers reconciliation, an answer to the problem of estrangement. Eph. 2:17-21. In this reconciliation God moves into the life of His very own. The believer is to enter-in-upon all that God has promised.

This provision is expressed from the standpoint of Christ as His baptizing the believer with the Spirit (Acts 1:5); it is expressed from the standpoint of the Spirit as His indwelling the life of the believer (Job 3:5, 6); and it is expressed from the standpoint of the believer as his being filled with the Spirit. Eph. 5:18. The believer is filled with the Spirit in proportion to the way he yields or surrenders to Him. The term filling could as well be translated possessed. The believer discovers that upon confessing Christ as Lord the Spirit of Christ interprets that lordship in his life. Rom. 8:14-16. Consequently life under the lordship of Christ is life in the Spirit, life permeated with the sanctifying influence of His presence, life bearing the "fruit of the Spirit"—love, joy, peace, long-suffering, gentleness, goodness, faith, meekness, and temperance. Gal. 5:20-22.

The ineffectiveness of the church is directly related to the failure to honor the Holy Spirit. We cannot do the Spirit's work apart from Him! Many persons are like the "dozen in the dark" described in Acts 19. As Paul detected a missing essential in both the men and their message, so there is something missing in the lives and witness of many so-called Christians today. The lack of victory, the absence of compassion, the complacency that haunts the brotherhood is present because we too often are satisfied to live after the flesh rather than in the Spirit. To share truly in the evangelistic role of the Spirit we must share in His fullness and power. We need to humble ourselves and seek Him. Satisfaction with our own abilities and arguments needs to be corrected by a yearning for His presence. Christ doesn't send us out to win arguments but to witness of an experience with Him. No one truly witnesses apart from a vital experience with the Holy Spirit!

Pentecost was the beginning of something to involve the whole world. Unless the church realizes this, it shuts itself up in a monologue. God is interested in the world—God made the world, Christ died for the world, Jesus as Lord rules over the world, He will judge the world, God wants to save the world. This means that the church is for the world, a salt to the earth, for the Spirit of God moves to save the world. There should be congruence between what He is doing for the world and in the church.

III. *The Spirit as Co-ordinator—Negotiating Right Contacts*

The soul winner is not doing his own work with the Spirit's help, but is obeying the Spirit in doing His work. As witnesses we depend upon the Spirit to lead us to persons with whom He has already been working. When the Spirit led Philip to speak to the Ethiopian on the road to Gaza, Philip found that he was witnessing to a man in whose life the Spirit had already been negotiating. Acts 8. The conversion of a sinner rarely comes in the first single instance of witness, but happens as a consequence of a series of spiritual impressions made upon that person. When we witness to individuals, we are adding our expression of faith to a treasury of other influences which the Holy Spirit uses to call the person to salvation. Because of this one can witness with confidence, knowing that every contact made in the spirit of Christian love is a success. One can also witness with the hope that the person you are contacting may be saved on the spot, for your word may be the final touch the Spirit needs to clinch the evidence. Evangelism is not to be thought of as a profession but as a spirit of life, a spirit of joy in the Lord, of satisfaction and purpose that becomes convincing to others.

One of the beloved soul winners of the twentieth century is Dr. Walter Wilson of Kansas City, Missouri. As a medical doctor and pastor, his life and writings express the romance of witnessing. His contacts have been contacts of love, communications of the love of Christ which convinces persons that they miss something vitally important in not knowing Christ. In his own testimony, Dr. Wilson says that his ministry was transformed when he discovered the difference between asking the Spirit to help him and offering his body as a temple for the Holy Spirit in willingness to help *Him*.

It is the Spirit who is evangelist: He knows the hearts, He can lead one to the right contacts, and He knows their problems and patterns of thought and can guide the witness to the best approach. We must beware of "Saul's armour," of ready-made arguments upon which we rely, and think in terms of the importance of the individual, of understanding the person, and listen for the *still small voice* who will guide us into the truth needed on that occasion.

All who observe the witness of Dr. Billy Graham, and see the evidence of God's hand upon him in both his ministry of the Word and in the response to the Gospel, are aware that there is more to this success than mass psychology. Mr. Graham's own testimony is an open acknowledgment of the anointing of the Holy Spirit upon this work of evangelism. The preaching ministry of the Word, where there is evident sincerity and relevance, is one of the most effective ministries by which the Spirit convinces men of truth. As persons whose thinking is saturated day in and day out with the commercials and entertainment of our times, sit for a solid hour and think through a message of the Gospel with the man presenting it, a spiritual therapeutic occurs. Such in a mass evangelism setting is just as valid as in a Sunday morning worship hour, so long as it is the Gospel which is communicated. In such a setting, modern man, retreating into the crowd in a loss of identity, is suddenly arrested by the Holy Spirit and brought face to face with a word from God.

In another manner there is a kindred emphasis in the work of Dr. Samuel Shoemaker, and the *Faith at Work* program. Shoemaker's writings on the anointing of the Spirit make a significant contribution to the thought of the Christian world on the importance of the Spirit's work. In a very significant way the fellowship gatherings are seeking to discover the power of spiritual fellowship to win others to Christ. The emphasis is upon the Spirit's role in creating the quality of fellowship that commends salvation through brotherhood.

One of the unique aspects of the Spirit's role is that of His anointing for spiritual insight. John writes, "But ye have an unction from the Holy One, and ye all know all things." The One who inspired the Scriptures also interprets them to the believer. By His inspiration the events of God's revelation received their interpretation through the writers. Now as we read the writings, the same Spirit interprets them to us. It is the inner witness of the Spirit which communicates Christ to the believer. In this sense the written Word has led to a depth awareness of the living Word, and the believer is taken beyond the letter of the Word into the life of the Spirit. Heb. 4:12, 13. The letter is the law, and it kills our pride and self-sufficiency. But it is inadequate, for it can only kill. II Cor. 3:1-6. To simply judge sin and expose it is not to correct it. "The letter killeth, but the Spirit giveth life." It is the life in the Spirit which truly expresses the nature of the divine kingdom. Rom. 14:17. The believer shares this life, and finds within the Scriptures a spirit of Scripture which is relevant and applicable in every time and situation. The role of the Spirit is dynamic, interpreting the most relevant message in the world in a manner understandable to all. I John 2:20, 27.

One of the most important matters in this discussion has been left for the conclusion of this chapter. If the Holy Spirit is "Lord of the Harvest," God's Evangelist in the world, God the Spirit moving in the world to win that world in love. It is inconceivable that a soul winner should work with such a Person and not communicate with Him. Since the Spirit is a Person, it is possible to talk with Him. Since He is God, we must talk with Him. The Bible speaks of the communion of the Holy Ghost, and it is hardly possible to have meaningful communion with a person apart from communication. II Cor. 13:14. Some persons have a theological block that prevents a discussion of praying to the Holy Ghost. In turn they ought to be asked about the validity of a theology that acknowledges a Triune God but refuses to communicate with the Triune expression.

The argument is often raised that Jesus, announcing the coming of the Spirit, said, "He shall not speak of himself; but whatever he shall hear, that shall he speak." From this it is concluded that the Spirit never speaking of Himself, is not One who would honor our prayers if addressed to Him. However, the Spirit by inspiring the Holy Scriptures did and does speak of Himself in the Bible!

The correct reading of the statement of Christ is that the Spirit will not speak *from Himself* but *from God,* a statement that affirms the unity of the work which Christ had completed with the work the Spirit would continue; the revelations of the Spirit which were to follow the earthly ministry of Christ would not be expressions of another program or purpose than that of the Father as revealed in Christ. Consequently the work of the Spirit glorifies Christ, for He interprets and applies what the Father has revealed and provided in the Son.

The Christian witness must of necessity share in a deep communion of the Holy Spirit. This is essential for the conforming of one's own life to the will and nature of Christ. It is also essential to sense day by day the leading of the Spirit in doing His work and in meeting those persons in whose lives He has been at work. Would you be a witness for Christ, a soul winner in the work of the kingdom? Begin by praying for His guidance:

Blessed Spirit of God, fill my life with Your presence, sanctify my thoughts and motives for the glory of Christ, empower me for effective witness, and lead me to the persons you want me to point to Christ today.

9

THE VICTORY OF
DEPTH PRAYER

*"For we wrestle not against flesh
and blood, but against principalities, against powers,
against the rulers of the darkness of this world, against
spiritual wickedness in high places." Ephesians 6:12*

The Holy Spirit does not work through methods but through men, not through programs but through personalities. E. M. Bounds reminds us: "The church is looking for better methods; God is looking for better men." One is properly disciplined for the task of soul winning when he is prayerfully disciplined to be a saint. The modern-day church is in need of saints, men committed wholly to the Lord, men whom the Spirit can use, men mighty in prayer. Paul's testimony must become ours: "Our sufficiency is of God; who also hath made us able ministers of the new testament; not of the letter, but of the Spirit: for the letter killeth, but the Spirit giveth life." Consequently our insufficiency is because we do not appropriate from God. Jas. 4:3. The preaching man must first be a praying man, a man whose life is a confession of absolute dependence upon God.

But prayer is not simply an act; it is an attitude. It is not simply a ritual; it is a relationship. Prayer is an interchange with God in the Spirit. It is the deep "communion of the Holy Ghost." The spiritual poverty that plagues our preaching, and the cold

orthodoxy that structures our theology, must give way to the
dynamic of the Spirit mediated in prayer. The awareness that
prayer is confessing relationship, is the sharing of love with the
One who is wholly other, creates a sense of divine presence in the
soul and thought of the believer. Eph. 4:13-21. Jesus said, "Without me ye can do nothing," and again, "If ye shall ask any thing
in my name, I will do it." Effective prayer is found only in the
feeling of absolute necessity and the faith that recognizes His will
and identifies with it.

Prayer is not overcoming God's reluctance; it is laying hold
on His willingness. Prayer is not talking God into doing something
He doesn't want to do; it is rather giving Him the moral right to do
what He has been wanting to do for a long time. Heb. 4:15, 16.
In His sovereignty, the aspect of His character which determines
the balance between His love and His wrath, between His mercy
and His justice, God has provided man a realm of freedom. Rather
than break forth in wrath against man's sin, God's sovereignty,
as an attribute of His character, tempers the wrath with love so
that He expresses Himself in patience. This patience is expressed
in the words, "The Lord . . . is not willing that any should perish,
but that all should come to repentance."

Consequently it is God's sovereignty that makes possible man's
freedom. Freedom is not the absence of law but the privilege which
certain laws make possible. Freedom would be impossible in an
unstructured universe, as it is impossible in a poorly structured
society.

Thus prayer is the expression of man's greatest freedom, the
freedom to invite God to function in a realm where His justice
has decreed that He will not move in by coercion. As shall be
discussed in this chapter, we live in a world "that lies in the lap
of the wicked one," a world under the influence of the demonic, and
it is our privilege to resist the devil by lifting our voices in prayer
to a sovereign God who can always move in, yet who does so
only when it can be by *permeation* rather than by *coercion*. The
message of the Incarnation and the Cross is the ultimate evidence
that God in His battle with Satan has defeated the devil, not by

coercive measures but by infinite condescension that exposed and expelled darkness by the permeation of light.

Some determinists think that if God knows what is best and will do it anyway, why pray? On the contrary, the Christian has discovered that just as God called him rather than coerced him to come to Christ, just so God works in the total thrust of the kingdom by calling rather than coercing. With the concept of sovereignty stated above (that which in the human realm is illustrated by a disciplined spirit), it follows that there is a realm of freedom where the degree in which the expression of the ultimate or highest will of God is limited to our prayers.

This means that intercessory prayer is not coaxing God into responding, but wrestling against the demonic, sharing with God in overcoming the hostile forces of "spiritual wickedness in high places" (Eph. 6:12). Importuning in prayer, or as the old saints expressed it, praying through, is getting through to God in the sense of moving beyond all the obstacles within and about us that hinder the Spirit of God. The condition of the soul, the consistency of one's fellowship, is a determining factor in the "time element" as well as the "depth element" in effective prayer. It has been said that "potency in prayer is not measured by the clock any more than power in preaching."

In His illustration of the man who went to his friend at midnight and asked for three loaves, Jesus presents a story that is correctly interpreted not from the story but from His conclusion. Rather than emphasizing that as this man was so importunate that he finally secured an answer, so we must continue to force our requests upon God, Jesus concludes the illustration by saying, "God isn't like that." He presents a God that can be known as a Father, as One who readily gives "the Holy Spirit to them that ask him" (Luke 11:13). Prayer is thus asking and receiving to find in His grace all that is needed for effective Christian living. Prayer is discovering God's will in His Word and promises, and then conditioning one's own soul to this will by affirming in prayer that this is what is most desired in one's life. I John 5:14, 15. Prayer is sharing in the Spirit who understands God's perfect will in a

manner so far beyond our own understanding that He makes intercession for us with a depth of yearning that cannot be expressed!
Rom. 8:26-28.

Prayer is sensing the opposition of the demonic to the work
of Christ and daring to defy the powers of evil which would oppress
the Christian by calling the divine to function in our realm. On
various occasions our Lord spent whole nights in prayer, not because He was not in full fellowship with God nor because God was
not pleased with Him fully enough to answer, but because He was
under the influence of all that it meant to be human and to be so
in a realm of demonic influences. He sought the presence of God
to certify that decisions He made were consistent with the divine
will and would consequently be expedited under the anointing of
the Holy Spirit. The Bible says that the Spirit was given without
measure unto Him, and it also says that He did always those things
which pleased the Father. This is prayer in depth—not simply
coming to God as a "rich uncle" from whom you can gain the
extra boost, but coming to the God of the universe before whom
you discover the true meaning of life. This is the risk of prayer—
one loses his own securities to find a greater security in God.

This experience of prayer in depth means giving up one's own
will, one's own wishes, and conforming one's self to the will of
Christ. To pray in His name is to give up all operations or plans
that are simply in your own name and to adjust your life to plans
that have His name over them. Prayer is thus costly. It is not
always comforting; it may be discomfiting. As with Paul in his
prayer for the removal of the "thorn in the flesh," so we discover
that prayer is surrender, giving up one's security in plans and purpose as self-conceived to find a greater security in Him whose
plan fills the universe. Prayer in depth is a victory over the world
within one, over the demonic without, and over circumstances
which tend to hide the face of God. Prayer is the soul reaching up
from a world under the perversion of sin to maintain contact with
the Saviour who is continually conquering sin!

I. *Prayer, the Triumph over the Demonic*

One of the questions regarding the role of prayer in evangelism is whether it does any good to pray for sinners? Those who hold that the only benefit of prayer is psychological—what it does in the person praying—can see no other benefit in intercessory prayer. This would mean that the benefit of prayer for the sinner is indirect, the benefit of conditioning the one praying to love and witness to that sinner. This is a valid contribution, but is not the total of the benefits of prayer in this respect. There are persons in need of prayer who do not pray for themselves. I John 5. The question is: Can the prayers of Christian people bring any more of the work of grace to bear upon their lives? From God's standpoint it must be said that there is no lack of love nor desire for the redemption of the sinner. To be consistent with the premises stated earlier in this chapter the validity of prayer for sinners must be seen in the largest possible perspective.

From the perspective of the problem of evil in the world and the manner in which God has chosen to triumph over it, we find God meeting Satan in conflict, not as a Sovereign using superior unlimited powers to throw him out, but as a God who condescends to meet him on the level of the lower being, man. Removing the power difference, the issue is now one of quality, of holiness against evil, of love against selfishness.

The classic example of this is the Incarnation of Christ, for in Jesus of Nazareth God became Man to overcome Satan by the quality of a holy life rather than by asserting superior powers. Doing so, Jesus said that He must first enter the strong man's house and bind the strong man, meaning that He penetrates the realm of Satan to overcome him. In His temptations Christ demonstrated that He would not use God—use the unlimited powers of the Eternal—for His own purposes, but would live the life of the eternal. Luke 4:1-14. Nearing the cross for the greatest of all conflicts between holiness and sin, between the divine and the demonic, Jesus said, "The prince of this world cometh, and hath nothing in me." Meeting all of the antagonism of Satan He an-

4

swered it by love. Absorbing the hostility sin produced in Himself unto the death, He thereby overcame it with love.

The method of God's victory over evil (the Incarnation and the Cross) is indicative of how God as Spirit overcomes the demonic today. He still penetrates the realm of the demonic through limited beings, simple men and women who are in fellowship with Himself. God's Spirit moves in and through men who believe, and upon others because we believe. As believers in the territory overrun by the demonic raise their voices in prayer, God answers, for such prayer gives Him the moral right to move in and answer! Now one who is a member of God's family, a citizen of heaven here in this world, an ambassador for Christ who represents His cause in an alien land, has called on his Sovereign! This is another aspect of intercessory prayer, that of defying Satan by deliberately calling on God. Daniel, the praying saint of the Old Testament, found that in his intercession he was wrestling against the prince of darkness. Dan. 9. Paul says that we "wrestle . . . against spiritual wickedness in high places."

It follows that not only does prayer do something for the one praying, but it is a deliberate defiance of the devil himself. Heb. 5:7-9. No wonder it has been said that the devil trembles when he sees the weakest saint upon his knees. If Satan can keep God's people from intercessory prayer, he can hold the front! In this conflict between the kingdom of darkness and the kingdom of light, he seeks to keep the soldiers of Christ's army from engaging in the fray. It is where men have moved in at the cost of spiritual engagement, of deliberate conflict with darkness, that the front has been moved ahead for Christ. At various times men sent to new beach-heads have been expendable—martyrs, who gave their lives willingly for the cause of Christ. Such martyrs believed that they were "filling up" in their own bodies the suffering of the Lord Jesus. Col. 1:27. Paul says, "All that will live godly in Christ Jesus shall suffer persecution."

There is an inner suffering that many of us draw back from— the suffering of giving up immediate self-interests and involving one's self in conflict with the realm of darkness—sharing the work of the Spirit in the conquest of new territory. Matt. 16:18, 19. We are too comfortable in this world, too satisfied in our own pursuits, and not deeply concerned about our fellows. Prayer in evangelism is the recognition that you can vindicate God in His bringing to bear upon such a sinner convictions that are not normally mediated by his circumstances or environment. Those of us who have been born within and nurtured inside the community of faith have such influences bearing upon our lives; persons lacking these influences need our prayers and our witness. As we thus move into enemy territory, the Spirit of God through our witness can reach that soul for the kingdom. James says, "Resist the devil," and he will back up. In fact, he will flee from you!

II. *Conditioning One's Self for the Spirit's Direction*

When we pray we should be aware that God may want to use us to help answer our own prayers. Praying for a sinner does not mean that God will convert that sinner apart from a witness through some member of the kingdom. It is at this point that the greater implication of prayer is seen in conditioning us to be led of the Spirit in His work. Jesus said, "If ye ask any thing in my name, I will do it." Far too often the requests which we bring to God can be brought only over our name. These He has not promised to answer. It is the request that is made in the name of Christ, that can be made over His signature, which He has promised to answer. Prayer thus involves the discernment of His will and the identification of one's life with His purpose.

Prayer conditions one's soul to sense the leading of the Spirit. It creates an attitude which is consistent with the Spirit of Christ and an atmosphere which is conducive to the Holy Spirit's promptings or impressions. In the Book of Acts we read about when the church leaders met in prayer at Antioch: "The Holy Ghost said, Separate me Barnabas and Saul for the work whereunto I have called them" (Acts 13:2, 3). When the Jerusalem Conference had considered the word Paul brought from Galatia of how the Spirit was working there and his request that they accept the more unorthodox procedures and thus maintain unity even though they lacked uniformity, the conference responded with the divine direction, "It seemed good to the Holy Ghost, and to us" (Acts 15:28)! Committee meetings in the life of the church should be no less Spirit-directed and Spirit-permeated than the worship service. Where God's people truly pray, God's Spirit will give a corresponding witness.

Living in an attitude of prayer implies a constant desire for the presence and grace of God in life's experiences. It also means a constant openness for the leading of the Holy Spirit, anticipating His promptings to contact the right persons and sensing His voice in reaching them with the right probings and answers. One prays because he senses his own need. In soul winning one prays in humble acknowledgment that the power to convict and convince a person to commit all to Christ is an inner spiritual power which does in the person's heart what the witness can only communicate to his mind. Zech. 4:6. There is an indefinable something in true Christian witness called unction, a sense of divine presence that communicates more than the mere words of invitation. We must seek this unction, ask for it, refuse to be satisfied without it, pray until we are caught up in the joy of it. Our witness is not mere verbalism but a communication of the presence of the living Christ Himself!

We need to be cautioned that we do not mistake earnestness for unction. One may be ever so earnest and sincere and yet not have the unction. There may be purpose, perseverance, and performance, and yet all this be done in the flesh without God in it. Divine unction is not synonymous with talents. It is not the gift of genius; it is not simply a "smooth-selling" personality. Divine unction is the anointing of the Holy Ghost which brings spiritual results through the humblest vessel. Many a well-trained seminarian fails to achieve what his training has fitted him for simply because he relies on training and talent rather than seeking the anointing of the Spirit. This unction comes upon the person separated unto God, sensitive to the will of Christ, and surrendered to the work of the Spirit. The presence of this unction makes minister or layman to be a flame for God. Although it is intensified to meet a given occasion, it is not simply an experience of the moment. It belongs to the whole of the man's life; it is the aura of divine presence over the whole of life. This gift of unction or anointing is conditional. It is dependent upon a spirit of prayer which engages the whole self in the work of the Spirit.

III. *Prayer Creates Compassion Which Truly Communicates*

The evangelist does not stand before the world with a spirit of condescending love, with the pride of privilege which reaches down to serve. He stands *among* his fellows pointing to the One in whom there is life. The second commandment is to love one's neighbor as one's self. Mark 12:31. If we open our lives to God in love, we also open our lives to what God would do in our fellows. Seeking to be neighborly or brotherly, we seek for them that which is most important in our understanding of life, relation with Christ. Regarding those outside of Christ as lost, we express our love by really caring, by a compassion that seeks to win them into the family of God. Such compassion is not worked up artificially; it must be truly felt by personal involvement.

There are several ways to experience compassion: one is to see the need of those around you until your own heart is moved in concern for them; another is to associate with someone who has loved ones or friends in distress. As Christians we learn compassion by opening our eyes to the distress and perversions of people in sin. An awareness of man's need produces compassion in the heart of the sincere Christian. But the second way to experience compassion is by living near to God, whose heart yearns for men in sin, longing for their salvation. Many saints who have never been privileged to move among downtrodden masses live with deep compassion and longing for their salvation, a compassion caught from the heart of God Himself. Compassion, gentleness, yearning over the souls of men—these one learns from God through the spirit of prayer. Some invalids have found a ministry of prayer that shares divine compassion in a depth that often surpasses that of active workers.

Communication of the Gospel is not simply a presentation of ideas. It is the communication of the love of God through the lives of those who know Christ. Many in sin could be won to the Saviour if they could be convinced that God really loves them—really cares! The Spirit of God is limited in His expression of this love to the tools He has to use—believers. Calvary stands in the center of history as the full proof of divine love. The believer communicates that love by evidencing the compassion of Christ to the world. Paul says, "We are ambassadors for Christ, as though God did beseech you by us: we pray you in Christ's stead, be ye reconciled to God." As we pray and draw near to God, He in turn draws near to us. Through us He communicates His love to the lost.

If we would become effective witnesses, we need this compassion. As we enter into the problems and lives of others, involving ourselves in their distresses, we do so with redemptive intent. To be effective we sit where they sit, we crawl into their skin, we experience the empathy that understands with concern. Prayerfully we negotiate the contact that expresses this love. It may be in music or word, in personal conversation, or the preaching mission. But regardless of the method, the message of love gets through. Warm hearts are born in prayer, and effective witnesses serve prayerfully.

10

THE STRATEGY OF
CONFRONTATION

"And unto the Jews I became as a Jew, that I
might gain the Jews; to them that are under the law,
as under the law, that I might gain them that are under
the law; to them that are without law, as without law,
(being not without law to God, but under the law to
Christ,) that I might gain them that are without law.
To the weak became I as weak, that I might gain the
weak: I am made all things to all men, that I might
by all means save some." I Corinthians 9:20-22

Information creates involvement. Truth may be accepted or
rejected, but in either case it has secured a response from the
person. When truth is personified, when it becomes personalistic
rather than merely moralistic, it demands response. Psychologically,
when a person is confronted by a person, he either gives him
acceptance or rejection. Christianity is such a confrontation, the
person of Christ confronting sinners and thereby requiring a response. Jesus said, "He that is not with me is against me; and he
that gathereth not with me scattereth abroad." The division is over
the person of Christ. Throughout His ministry, John writes, "There
was a division among the people because of HIM" (John 7:43).
Having affirmed that Jesus was not simply a teacher telling man
about God, but was God who came to teach, it follows that the
claims of Christ are the most divisive claims in the universe. He
expressed it in the words, "Think not that I am come to send peace
on earth: I came not to send peace, but a sword" (Matt. 10:34).
The call of grace comes through a confrontation with Jesus Christ,
an encounter that solicits involvement.

This chapter, which deals with methodology, properly follows the discussion of compassion, the spirit of love in communication. For where compassion is experienced, method will be found. Without compassion method is merely a shell without content, machinery without power, organization without life. But compassion only expressed in the prayer meeting will never save the world. That experience of involvement in Christ which communicates to the believer the "love of the Spirit" must in turn be communicated to the world. The Bible says that God loved the world. So must we. Again it says that Christ loves the world; He died for it. We become the channel through which He continues to express that love. The Spirit loves the world, and has been involving Himself in its problems for centuries, but love is communicated through personalities, persons through whom the Spirit expresses His concern. Methodology in evangelism teaches us how to confront persons, not only with convincing facts, but with comforting faith! When Jesus called His disciples, He immediately "began to send them forth" (Mark 6:7).

Methodology in the life of the church must be consistent with its essential nature. Methods that manipulate people, that violate the ethics of Christianity, or that magnify the personnel rather than the Saviour are improper. Such methods are of the flesh rather than the Spirit. Far too often persons working in the program of the church have borrowed the world's methods and tried to sanctify them at points where the methods violate Christian principles. But on the other side the church has sometimes been too slow to borrow good methods from the world that can be used in a way consistent with Christian ethics. Jesus said that often "the children of this world are . . . wiser than the children of light" (Luke 16:8). Above all, methods must be personal rather than impersonal, methods that communicate the spirit of Christian love, and through which the Spirit may express His compassion.

Out of a dozen years of evangelistic preaching missions or crusades in which almost every method possible has been utilized, the writer has sensed that methods of personal involvement are far superior to a more mechanistic method. Methods that treat a person impersonally, as an "it," do not carry the same influence as the more personal involvement. This is not to say that the Spirit has not far exceeded the method in calling persons to Christ. Many individuals have been converted by a tract, or by picking up a Gideon Bible in a hotel room. But even here the full joy of confession is realized only when they share their faith with another.

The preaching mission of evangelism, be it in a congregation or in a mass-meeting fashion, is one of the most potent methods of evangelism—a method in which persons who have retreated into the crowd in loss of identity are suddenly singled out by the Spirit and made aware that they are responsible persons under God. Such persons listening to the Gospel are able to identify when the truth is presented effectively. But even here, effective as this method is, the audience is made up of persons brought there by individual believers who have contacted them. It is evident, therefore, that evangelism is not simply the work of the clergy, but is the engagement of the total congregation. Evangelism is not the work of one man, not the oratory of an evangelist. It is the work of the body of Christ, the total involvement of the total brotherhood to reach the total community!

I. *Creativity in Discovering Approaches*

We are working with persons, not machines or animals. While much of a person's behavior may be predicted if one understands their pattern of thought and orientation in life, there is the variable in every person. Knowing how people think, what determines their actions, is imperative in a strategy of method. There is a sense in which the Christian witness must outsmart sinners! As strategists we should engage the person we contact in dialog, for by listening we may discover his yearnings as well as thought patterns. Beyond this we watch for the variable, seeking contact with the person's heart, the real source of his behavior. The Spirit can endow one with a gift of discernment to overcome the barriers erected against Christ. This divinely given wisdom enables the witness many times to use approaches that speak to the sinner in a manner far beyond human planning.

It has been said that "most noteworthy experiments in evangelism are almost without exception . . . the result of the initiative of some individual group of individuals who, in obedience to the inspiration of the Holy Spirit, start something new." It is often true that by the very nature of organization the leaders in a church movement become completely involved in the work of administration and fail in the work of evangelism. Is it not strange that in a brotherhood of believers the life of the church should become a status or system rather than a spirit? Organization is necessary, but it should not be placed over against evangelistic work in an either/ or matter. It is both/and! Consequently, the history of the church is a trail filled with new movements breaking off the side because laymen felt the church was "dead" and took hold of the task themselves, often resulting in a new group which repeated the cycle. Church groups have always tended to go through a cycle of warm enthusiastic acceptance of the Gospel, then to institutionalization, and then to a worship of the past. How far better if we would erase the degrees of difference between the clergy and the laity, and create a brotherhood in which we share fully together.

As the Sunday school has become a significant part of the life of the church, likewise the series of evangelistic meetings and other methods can be developed and utilized by the brotherhood. Fellowship evangelism, visitation evangelism, family evangelism, office evangelism (especially at coffee breaks), and cell-group evangelism all can be utilized by the members of a congregation.

The advantages of methods such as these are in the personal involvement which they entail and the fact that the whole brotherhood may share in them. Methods such as the preaching mission, radio, television, or religious film releases are more specialized and limit the participation. If we are to be effective in evangelism today, we need to engage the entire brotherhood, which in turn will penetrate the multitude of vocational worlds which they represent. Far too many professing Christians are spectators instead of being in the playing field. The church is not really the church until the center of its life is in balance with the circumference of the total brotherhood.

It is not the purpose of this book to deal with practices of evangelism as much as principles. Practices are multiple and vary in communities and cultures. Some methods are occasional and particular, while others are perennial and general. The Spirit uses a multitude of methods to meet each individual with a witness of grace in a complex stream of humanity. Our tendency is to become sold on one method and then spend our time defending it and criticizing others instead of seeing that the Spirit endows persons differently. As good stewards we each play in our place recognizing that in different roles we are on the same team. When we yield ourselves to the Spirit, the Lord of the Harvest, and share His compassion, method is simply the best way to reach our objective. It is especially true in evangelism that the means to an end should never be regarded as the end. The critique on much of modern evangelism expressed in the story of *The Gospel Blimp* is an exposure of this mistake.

II. *A Methodology that Is Flexible—Servant Rather Than Master*

Living things cannot be confined in static molds; they must break forth in expression. The living church, created by the inner witness of the Spirit, is a living, dynamic fellowship. Such a brotherhood is of necessity skeptical of the routine and desirous of renewal. But a congregation that quenches the Spirit soon finds that it is not true to its essential character, and Christ must say to it, "Thou hast a name that thou livest, and art dead." Methods like committees can multiply until they become accretions, and like barnacles on a boat may not only retard its progress but result in its ruin. For some years there was a sign on the Alaska highway, "Choose your rut well, you'll be in it the next twenty-five miles!" This might be said to some church groups that have been stuck with a few routine methods for years. We seem to forget that our choice of methods expresses our character.

The church cannot afford to let methods become masters; methods must be servants. Some serve a purpose for a time and need to be discarded. Others may last in effectiveness over the years, the latter being illustrated by the effectiveness of genuine worship experiences. Slavery to method can render any group so obsolete that the Gospel they present is unappealing because of the method involved. We tend to regard the organizational structure of a congregation or conference as the church. But the church is persons, the community of believers made up of laymen and ministers, not simply structure. The church is not enslaved by the routine nor by methods when it is yielded and sensitive to the creative work of the Spirit. We who believe are the church, and upon us rests the responsibility to discover the mind of Christ through the Word and Spirit. Ours is the commission and the mission of communicating Christ to the world. Paul wrote that to the Jew he became as a Jew, to those under the law as under the law, that he might by all means save some! Our adjustments of program and our additions of relevant methods find their directive and balance in Paul's words. Being all things to all men is not for the sake of selfish advantages of being at home in the world but sanctified adjustments to penetrate that world with the Gospel of Christ.

Many times our skepticism about methods other men are using with success is due to our limited understanding of their work or our lack of deep involvement in the work itself. After visiting the Billy Graham Crusade in Los Angeles, Dr. Helmut Thielicke wrote a reply which appeared in *Christianity Today,* October 25, 1963. Dr. Thielicke evidenced a spirit of humility and honesty as he stated the convictions which gripped him in the meeting. He was impressed with the Biblical content of the messages, and the careful way in which Graham called persons forward to "confirm their decision." His response was that "it became lightning clear that men want to make a decision, and that the meditative conversation . . . is only a poor fragment. . . . Once in their life they have perceived what it is like to enter the realm of discipleship. And if only this memory accompanies them, then that is already a great deal. But it would certainly be more than a memory. It will remain an appeal to them, and in this sense it will maintain its character *indelibilis.*"

But in addition to this analysis Dr. Thielicke stated a confession that should be made by many of us for the way in which we evaluate the methods of others. "It has been very easy for me to determine what was wrong or lacking in the other person. When I have been asked now and again about your preaching. . . . I have certainly not been too modest to make one or two more or less profound theological observations. . . . The question should be asked in the reverse form: What is lacking in me and in my theological colleagues in the pulpit and at the university lectern, that makes Billy Graham so necessary?" Thielicke's answer is a recognition of the various gifts of the Spirit functioning within the body of Christ in complementary and mutually expanding relationship, an insight which should lead us to gratitude for the brother with other gifts who shares in the larger work of the church.

Paul's word to the church at Rome applies to us in this area of differing methods. "Who art thou that judgest another man's servant? to his own master he standeth or falleth" (Rom. 14:4). In humble dedication each of us must seek the leading of the Spirit for methods that will enable us to confront others effectively with a witness of Christ.

III. *Witness-Confrontation—the Goal Which Judges Method*

The goal of confrontation, of penetration of society, is witness. The world about us needs to be confronted with the evidence of the Chirst-event in our lives. We seem to have little trouble getting ourselves involved in social realms of our interest. Evangelism is simply using this involvement for redemptive purposes. The church, made up of members who serve in a multitude of vocational and social worlds, is able to penetrate all of society with a witness of Christ. Methods of operation are determined by this goal of witness. Wherein methods do not result in witness, they are judged or condemned by the goal which they fail to reach. We must respect the law that certain practices will achieve a definite goal determined by the nature of the practices.

Preaching as prophetic utterance is one of the unique manners of witness in the Christian community. However, preaching that is simply a lecture on moral principles or social obligations, important as those may be, is not witness until it speaks of what the living Christ is doing to transform those areas. Biblical preaching is the prophetic utterance, the word of one who so lives in the Word and the Spirit that he voices anew the Word of God. Such preaching is a communication of the Gospel to the intent of persuasion. It is evangelistic preaching. The Christian ministry needs the unction of the Spirit to produce preaching from the heart of God. Only such preaching is truly the witness of Christ. The work of the ministry is unique. It is not simply teaching; it is teaching with a plus, the plus of divine anointing. Under this anointing preaching becomes a witness that moves men to decision. Our preaching of the Gospel stands under the judgment of its highest goal, the witness of the risen Christ.

Methods used also stand under this judgment, as to whether they are getting the witness through. Far too often so-called evangelistic meetings, in large gatherings or in cell groups, are only a gathering of believers who make the mistake of thinking that when they have discussed something they have done something. Real love for persons in the problems of sin is expressed only by our involving ourselves in the work of helping them. Loving one's neighbor as oneself points directly to this evangelistic witness. Many pastors have found that a well-planned visitation program—organizing and sending out members of the congregation in teams—is one of the effective methods, and is consistent with the goal of witness. A congregation which involves the total membership in such an enterprise strengthens itself, multiplies its outreach, and adds new believers to its membership. Jesus Himself sent out His disciples two by two, crossing social, political, racial, and class barriers with a witness that won persons from every walk of life to the Saviour.

Let us be humble enough to seek better methods, and sensitive enough to sense the Spirit's direction in utilizing them. The creativity of the Spirit functions in the multiple gifts of the brotherhood. Where there is consecration in depth, the sharing of divine purpose, the same Spirit who communicates His compassion through us will lead us to methods of witness. Our greatest need is an obedient response to Him. With this obedience there are guidelines of Christian ethics which preserve the moral values necessary in interpersonal relations. The search for effective methods must be accompanied by the sanctity of life which purifies the method. Regardless of how given persons feel they should get the task accomplished, the penetration must demonstrate the highest respect for personality and communicate a true sense of love, of compassion, learned from the Spirit of Christ.

As one seeks to witness in what is called personal evangelism, he will find every contact with his fellow man an opportunity. The approach is not to buttonhole each person and preach a young sermon, but to seek in normal dialog to express the joy of life in Christ in such a way as to capture the other person's interest and communicate an invitation to faith. Persons who share in visitation evangelism will plan an effective schedule of calling on homes with the express purpose of inviting them to the Christ-life. Cell-group evangelism communicates through the dialog of group discussions, utilizing the group dynamics which make such a setting significant.

Methods of evangelism that are identified with the social aspects of the Gospel must also communicate a witness of Christ and not simply a call to a better status in life. One does not only seek to take people out of the slums, but to take the slum out of people. For example, rescue mission work is most effective where it regards sin as sin rather than simply an illness, and leads the person to new hope by discovering that his problem is not an incurable perversion, but one common to all men which can be corrected by the Spirit of Christ. The work among the gangs in many of our cities reveals that the depth cure for dope addiction is the indwelling of the Holy Spirit, just as the cure for their violence in conquest of status is by the acceptance to be found in Christ and His disciples.

Periodically a community needs a co-operative evangelistic mission, often referred to as "mass evangelism." Since the writer has engaged in this type of evangelistic mission for the past ten years across the States, Canada, and other parts of the world, it is presented here with the conviction that this is one of the relevant and effective methods. The remarkable work of the Graham Crusades is undisputably one of the most significant thrusts of evangelism at the grass roots of life in this century. There are many benefits of this type of work, among them being the fact that all of the preceding methods referred to are either incorporated in a full-scale program or contribute to it. Some of these benefits are the following: (1) Co-operative evangelism in a community magnifies the Gospel of Christ above the denominational reputation of the various churches of the community. (2) Co-operative evangelism proves that the church regards Jesus Christ as greater than any system of religion or structure of doctrine, and defies the idolatry of identifying the kingdom of Christ solely with some particular denomination, thereby creating a greater understanding of the essential issues in the mind of the unbeliever. (3) Co-operative evangelism enables us to confront modern man with the Gospel where he is, in view of the fact that sociologists and psychologists describe modern man as retreating into the crowd. (4) Co-operative evangelism strengthens the churches of a community by uniting them in a total effort of witness, and by training scores if not hundreds of counselors who in turn enrich the life of their own congregation in the years following. (5) Co-operative evangelism utilizes the benefits of the multiple year-around programs of evangelism being perused in the congregation, and in doing so provides added incentive for them in their ongoing program.

But it must here be emphasized that it is the quality of such a program that is important rather than simply its size. Such a program calls for sound policies, consistent personnel, careful and fair financial planning through a local committee, honest and understanding presentations of the Gospel in the midst of doctrinal differences, procedures of invitation that refuse to trick or manipulate persons and that are consistent with the essential nature of the Gospel and the church, and by advance work guided by personnel representing the team that will be involved. Such a program when handled well can enhance the public image of the church. On the other hand, such a program run by persons with a closed system that exploits the public can destroy confidence in the church. One of the greater tests of Christian community is whether a community of pastors and visiting team can demonstrate by mutual understanding and adherence to the highest principles the true character and values of the Christian faith.

It should be noted that this is co-operation, not identification. Such sharing can result in the rethinking and deepening of our convictions as we associate with those who interpret their experience with Christ from a different orientation. The Christian church, wherever it has been truly Christian, has always had an ecumenical spirit. However, the current movement for a federated church as a world-wide ecumenical organization is a different matter. This is a movement which cannot be ignored, for we have many Christian brethren who are expressing their mission through this channel; but at the same time it is a movement which dare not be idolized until we sacrifice the values of interpretations of the Gospel which as denominations we have been able to express. No group has captured the kingdom, and no group can or will contain it, even the ecumenical movement of our time. As Dr. Thielicke stated while in New York City, the present "ecumenical movement stands in danger of becoming a bureaucracy." So far the depth issues of the Reformation have not been adequately recognized in the movement. The work of evangelism must not be redirected into becoming a program to create a power structure by winning persons from group loyalties to organizational loyalty. Ours is the call to win men to Christ, to open our lives to what God is doing in our neighbor (friend or enemy), and witness to a unity of the faith that transcends cultural, national, and denominational lines. This unity is a matter of spirit, not of status; it is the unity of the "in Christ" relation spoken of by our Lord in His high-priestly prayer. John 17. As a unity of spirit, of attitude, of confessing that truth grips us rather than that we embody it, this unity is created by the Holy Spirit and can and should exist amidst denominational differences. Keeping our goal clear we must not be sidetracked from our one primary mission.

As in any area of achievement, there is a sense in which each of us is first of all an apprentice. To become an effective soul winner we live close to God in learning from Him, and close to men in understanding how to converse with them. The first rule, then, as a guide to become an effective witness is simply to begin. R. A. Torrey, writing on personal evangelism, emphasizes this as the first step, "Begin." When we pray the Lord of the Harvest to thrust forth laborers into His harvest, we will find Him answering through us.

11

THE MODERN MAZE

*"This know also, that in the last
days perilous times shall come. For men
shall be lovers of their own selves . . .
lovers of pleasures more than lovers of
God; having a form of godliness, but denying the
power thereof." II Timothy 3:1-5*

The modern world is often characterized by the word "escapism." Man seeks to escape his real problem by turning to the pursuit of pleasure. The result of this is the self-centeredness that in turn destroys life. The paradox of pursuing happiness is that in doing so one does not find happiness . . . one finds that happiness is a by-product, a benefit of pursuing holiness. Christianity does not simply seek to cure the problems we have; it seeks to cure the problem that we are—persons who like sin. In correcting the depth problem Christ leads us in a way of holiness which is supremely enjoyable. Man has constantly sought his answers elsewhere, within his own sphere; and in the resultant confusion he fails to find God's answer. Modern man forgets that his sin is basically against God, and he seeks an inferior way of correction. We have turned the psychiatrist's couch into a modern confessional. Consequently, someone has said we are so confused we are running to the psychiatrists until they are so confused they are running to each other!

Our age brings us to the apex of humanistic achievement. We have inherited influences that have complicated the issue. Since the rise of sociology, through the work of Comte, man has social-ized everything, even God. In the development of the theory of evolution Darwin's successors have even evolutionized morals. As a result of Einstein's challenges, it appears man has made every-thing relative, including truth. Modern man regards everything as relative, denying an absolute, resulting in man doing that which is "right in his own eyes." There are numerous attempts to bring order out of chaos. Existentialism seeks to make life meaningful apart from obedience to the Word of God. Communism seeks to direct man's struggle for food away from his hunger for God. Internationalism attempts to erect a human society that will not commit suicide. And religionism seeks to salvage world peace through a revival of religion. Even the latter is inadequate, for it is an attempt to use God for human ends, rather than to surrender to His sovereign will. The tendency to equate Christianity and Americanism has retarded the progress of the kingdom, for the idolizing of any particular political or cultural system is to place one's security in a transient power. The God who shatters idols will do so again.

In the philosophical realm humanism has robbed men of faith in the supernatural. Man's faith is in man and his discoveries. In the moral realm self-centeredness decrees the behavior, and the center of personality has shifted from the spirit to the flesh, resulting in unbridled lust for status, material security, and the perversions of sensuality. Our advertising system is largely dominated by depth psychologists whose appeal is to the "lust of the flesh, and the lust of the eyes, and the pride of life" (I John 2:17). Even the political realm is often motivated by economic advantages instead of moral and spiritual principles. The Christian church claims to have an answer, but within its membership there is little deep par-ticipation and loyalty.

Professor Martin of Cornell College has said, "American men-tality is simply not geared for deep spirituality." Our unwillingness to go deeply with God renders the Christian church weak and anemic. Although the entire brotherhood of the church should be deeply committed to Christ, many church members know nothing of a personal conversion and vital relationship with Him. This means that the Christian witness, the soul winner, is an exception when he ought to be the rule! But rather than be discouraged by this the true Christian ought to realize his advantage. The born-again Christian who truly witnesses (rather than brags about his experience) has the advantage of speaking from an experience in which he is personally involved. We need to remember that many persons lost in the maze of modern life may be well educated in particular fields and yet be in kindergarten theologically.

To reach the modern man we need to discover the things that motivate him. As pointed out in the chapter on ethics "modern man is characterized by three things, anomi, anonymity, and alienation." Anomi, the loss of ethical standards, leaves man with no absolute, no moral laws or consciousness of guilt. Anonymity means the loss of personal identity, of personal worth, until man retreats into the crowd and becomes "the mass man," "the organization man." Alienation refers to man's isolation, the hostility, and the loneliness of the soul walled off from others in its split-level trap. To understand modern man we need to go beyond Freud in asking of the emotional and glandular factors that create his neuroses, and ask with Jung what it is the person is dodging in the here and now. We go beyond Jung, for the Christian faith can help a man to be realistic, to face life honestly, to cease trying to escape from himself by turning to God. In Christ the false-self that has betrayed every man, that old man under the reign of sin, is crucified and a new self is born, a self "renewed in knowledge after the image of him who created [us]" (Col. 3:10).

I. *The Challenge of the Population Explosion*

This is one of the most significant times in the history of mankind for various reasons, not the least of which is that of the multitudes of people that inhabit the globe at one time. It is said that because of plagues, war, famine, and disease, the total population of the world did not reach one billion at a given time until 1831. By 1931 the population doubled, reaching two billion. By 1961 that population reached nearly three billion, and it is estimated that by the year 2000 it will reach seven billion. The social, economic, and political issues of such a multiplied population are beyond our imagination. That which concerns us directly at this point is the implications of this for evangelism. Such a population explosion means that proportionately the Christian population becomes increasingly smaller. Thus the number of Christian witnesses becomes increasingly less prominent. This calls for the utilization of effective methods of communication coupled with carefulness that the need for greater outreach does not prevent quality.

Another facet of the problem is seen in the multiplication of needs in a society where man's sinfulness is expressed by increasing perversity in the mass. Dr. Niebuhr has pointed out that the mass is more corrupt than the individual. As the population multiplies, the directives for behavior become more that of the mass, of the status quo of the larger group. Individual convictions, which answer to God's Word, are displaced by the conventions of the group. With this shift of authority and the denial of the authority of the Scripture, there follows the continual lowering of moral standards and the increase of violence. Truly "in the last days perilous times shall come" (II Tim. 3:1). Witnesses for Christ may find a return of persecution as man's perversions increase and the hostilities toward the witness of the Gospel increase correspondingly.

Obviously the problems that concern the sociologist in resolving the many difficulties in the social and economic aspects of life concern the Christian witness also. The challenges for social involvement in working with the problems of suffering, of deprivation, and of crime must not be minimized. The church is both a conscience to the world, and also a healing agent, binding up the wounds, comforting the afflicted, and feeding the hungry. Yet these will continue to be never-ending problems, and the church must keep clear its message in serving them by answering the basic problem, calling persons to a life in Christ, the quality of which will offer a lasting contribution in the other areas of need. The church must keep its basic mission clear, and then move from that basic premise to the various expressions of grace through which the church gives itself in service.

II. *The Awakening of World Religions*

These are days in which the Gospel is in dispute. The perplexities of our age have stirred anew the questions after the meaning of life and human destiny. The world-wide communication has increased understanding between religious faiths. There is a new liberalism that sees God at work in many of the world religions in ways that claim to bring people to salvation. This concept is inconsistent with the basic evangelical premise of the exclusiveness of the work of Christ. Holding to the belief that "God was in Christ, reconciling the world to himself" Christendom has affirmed that Christ is God. This means that He is the way of salvation, and not one among many. However, just as persons in pre-incarnation days were saved through the work purposed by God in Christ without being clear on its meaning in details, so it is conceivable that persons today may come to salvation through Christ's work while not being able to verbalize it in detail. But this is not to say that we do not try to evangelize the Jews or Moslems, since they believe in the one sovereign God. These must be led to see how this one Sovereign God has disclosed Himself fully in Christ. The rejection of Christ is the rejection of the character and content of the revelation in Scripture. However verbalized, what is offered as the way of salvation must be consistent with what we know in Christ.

In our time the multiple religions of the world are stirring with new life. The Moslem and Buddhist religions are sending missionaries to all parts of the world. Communism is a heresy from Christianity, and is a religion for millions of persons. The rise of Bahaism, the spread of the numerous cults, and the development of a new religion in Japan which has grown to ten million adherents in a few years is further evidence of this religious stirring. The Christian witness is facing a most difficult mission. If it is simply religion we are promoting, there is an abundance of this in the world. If it is encouragement to greater ethical concern, there is common ground here with numerous religions. The success of the Christian mission depends upon the clarity with which we com-

municate relationship with the risen Christ above mere religious
ideas. But reaching persons of other faiths is not a simple matter.
One cannot be naive and uninformed. On the contrary, the Christian witness should study another religion until he discovers its
appeal, until he could be tempted to join it; then he will know what
it is that must be answered by the Christian faith. This is a risk,
the risk of evangelism, but just as in higher education or other
areas, this is a calculated risk.

A significant function of evangelism is that of exposing false
faiths, whether they be those of the agnostic, atheist, cultic, or
animistic persuasions. Although a witness does not dogmatically
attempt to coerce a person into belief in Christ, he does deliberately
seek to expose the inadequacy of his position. Multitudes of persons are comfortable where they are, and satisfied with their own
thought or religion. Just as Jesus challenged the religious persons
of His day, calling them to a new faith by exposing the inadequacy
of what they had through a presentation of something better, so we
follow His example in meeting the various religious positions of
our day. A rise of religions is an opportunity to evangelize, for in
such a time people are thinking and searching for meaning and may
be inclined to be more receptive to the Christian witness. We need
the vision of Christ to recognize even in such difficult situations
opportunities that can be turned to the advantage of the kingdom.
As Christian witnesses we must beware lest we become lost in the
modern maze, or defeated by our own fears and insecurities. The
effective witness is one who knows security in Christ.

III. *Suburbia and Its Pressures to Conform*

A new mentality and a new cultural pattern characterizes our
age. The idolatry of the peer group has filled the place of old-
fashioned Christian virtue and service. We are more concerned
about status than saintliness, about the will of the peer group than
the word of prophets. Not only have we confused our moral principles until the white has merged with the black to issue in gray,
but that gray scowl on the face of a disapproving set makes us wilt
and fall in line. We are obsessed by fear, the fear of being differ-

ent, and the pressures to conform make us puppets rather than
men. The nonconformist, the man who stands for principles of
truth, honesty, and purity, finds himself the object of ridicule and
rejected by those who place prestige above personal worth. Consequently, few persons think for themselves, few arrive at convictions that stabilize and enrich their lives, and few live redemptively
in society. Instead of being persons with a vision of God, a sense
of purpose, and a clear course of behavior modern man is like the
rat in the psychologist's laboratory, seeking its way through the
maze in search of some tidbit. But the human maze is even more
confusing, for there are no permanent forms or lasting principles
by which a person can move to a determined goal. In the modern
maze man finds himself in danger of being trampled under in his
very quest for meaning.

There is evidence of this even in the Christian realm, where
the believers should have a sense of conviction, a clarity of vision,
and a commitment to discipleship. But rather than this certainty,
multitudes of so-called Christians in churches and colleges describe
themselves as "searching." This could be an expression of humility, meaning we are seeking ways of strategy and depths of insight
to make us more effective, but too often it means that the contemporary church is lost itself and its committee meetings are not to
discover how to expedite the program of mission but are gatherings
to discover what we should be about! We must regain a sense of
Christian mission.

Rather than to announce that Christ came "to seek and to save
that which was lost" (Luke 19:10), we argue about what it means
to get saved. Instead of believing that the "new birth" can send
a new man into society as a transforming influence, we spend much
of our time discussing the social aspects of the Gospel and find
ourselves parroting the self-diagnosis of our society. We seem to
be lost ourselves, lost in a maze of uncertainty and indecision. We
gather pastors from churches in urban settings to discuss urban
evangelism and never check on what they are actually producing in
their congregations. So often we pool our own ignorance and come
up with nothing, or incorporate the man diligent enough to be doing

something for Christ in a group whose bias serves to squelch individual initiative. If there is any method that will work in the modern maze, any prophetic utterance that will pierce the peer group, or any comprehension that will truly communicate Christ, it will be found solely by the creative guidance of the Holy Spirit. II Tim. 1:2.

The modern church is not in need of new insights half as much as a renewal of enthusiasm. The early Christians had a Christ to confess, a creed to believe, and a song to sing, and their enthusiasm was contagious. The martyrs who went singing to their stakes demonstrated that there is sustaining grace that is personally mediated by the Spirit of Christ independent from the support of a peer group. The experience of faith that truly satisfies will sell itself in our age. If someone gave you a diamond as big as a dime you'd show it to everyone: if you really come to an appreciation of the "riches of grace" in Christ Jesus you will share this with joy! In conversation persons talk of things that are of primary interest. We will begin conversing of Christ among today's lost souls whenever we bring the reality of Christ into our conversations as Christians.

Men who will move the world are men not moved by it. Once we have found victory over the world within us, we can carry our vision to the world about us. John writes, "This is the victory that overcometh the world, even our faith" (I John 5:4), a victory that he interprets as overcoming the world within us which chafes at God's commandments. Once the first victory is won, the inner victory, and we no longer find God's commandments grievous, the second victory over the world without is certain. One who delights in God's will does not find it difficult to move in a world motivated by a lesser will with a victory that speaks to it rather than become enslaved by it. The Christian witness is the demonstration of the quality of life with Christ, a witness which recommends this life to the unsaved. To become a Christian is not to take a naive or inferior position, but to enter into a life that is of the greatest quality and satisfaction. As witnesses we move in a perplexed society with the poise and purpose of those who walk with God.

One of the motifs that strengthens the Christian witness is that of eschatology. We believe that God is working out His purpose in history, and that His purpose will come to a grand victorious climax. As the martyrs for the faith of Christ saw their sacrifice as a necessary part of the triumph of grace over the demonic, so we must regard the risk and cost of evangelism as a part of the price of ultimate victory. Soldiers give themselves for an ideal which many of them will never live to see, how much more the Christian soldier in the spiritual warfare in which we are all engaged should give himself to bring to fulfillment that ultimate victory. God's program will not be defeated—as He has promised a restoration of all things, so He will fulfill it. Rom. 8:18-39. Ultimately His purpose will permeate the universe, and both heaven and hell will acknowledge His holiness and His sovereignty. But this victory is of the character of permeation rather than coercion, to the end that the rebels of hell will not be able to dig up one valid attack upon God's program though they have an eternity to try it.

The story is told of an American tourist in Russia, who was asked by a communist, "Have you read Karl Marx?" Upon the tourist's affirmative reply, the communist expressed his deep convictions in his answer, "Then you know how it is going to come out." If that tourist had been, or was, a Christian he should have asked, "Have you read the Bible?" and followed with the same answer, "Then you know how it is going to come out!" The theology of the Bible is saturated with divine purpose; we can interpret the end from the middle. As Christians we know how it is going to end: we stand on the victory side of the cross. Each civilization and government, American, Russian, and all, is only temporary, not eternal. The eternal kingdom will someday look back upon this time in history as a mere speck along the line of God's over-all purpose. This is our faith and our strength; we are not one-world beings but persons created for two worlds.

When Adoniram Judson went to Burma with the Gospel he was beset with the most severe difficulties. The Gospel was rejected. He was persecuted and imprisoned. For seven years this opposition continued, increasingly discouraging from afflictions on the field and from the despair of the home mission board. He was in and out of prison at least four times. On one occasion he was so emaciated when released that even his wife failed to recognize him. This man was tried to the full. After seven years of this, with no converts to the faith, Judson received a letter from the home board begging him to acknowledge the futility of continuing and to return home. His testimony in reply reveals the reason why he finally conquered and built a church in Burma, and how we can build the church in our day: "The future is as bright as the promises of God!"

These are crucial days, days in which men have died for their faith, days in which men who live their faith are tried by multiple temptations. The church is commissioned to be the salt of the earth, and the light of the world. As the body of Christ, the redemptive arm which the Lord stretches out across the world, the church experiences the continuation of the cross. As Christians we deliberately create tension by lifting up Christ before a world that prefers to be its own god, and absorbing this tension in witnessing love that continues beckoning men to the Saviour. Should hostility increase, and the powers of the demonic be released against the church in persecution, we should find in divine grace the power to live and die nobly for His cause and glory. Should privileges continue to be granted the church to carry on its ministry unharried, we need even more grace to live each day without compromise, being witnesses by our position in Christ. The prayer of Hans Langmantel of South Germany, shortly before being beheaded for his faith in Christ, in 1529, is a fitting conclusion for a book on evangelism and discipleship:

"O God, our heavenly Father, come with the power of Thy Holy Spirit . . . preserve us in Thy keeping, that we may not faint and abandon Thy Word. Let us enjoy the faithfulness which Thou hast shown us through Thy Son Jesus Christ; and in order that we may always earnestly contemplate this, send us Thy Holy Spirit, and kindle in us the fire of Thy divine love; lead us, Thou who didst teach it in deed, that we may also exercise ourselves therein, and observe and practice it as Thy dear children, that this gift may come upon us, and that, even as we are called, we may by it order our lives in this Thy truth, maintain peace and unity, and love one another in truth with a pure heart.

"To this end, O God, let the light of Thy divine glory illuminate us, that we may walk in it. O Lord, keep us in it as Thy dear children, and let us never become obscured by the abominable darkness of this world, which has gained the upper hand with all unfaithfulness, and which will be followed by death. . . .

"O God, we beseech Thee for one thing more: Send us to this end Thy Holy Spirit, endue us with His power, renew our hearts, and make us strong in Thee, that we may obediently hear Thee in Thy obedience, and praise Thy name. . . . In Christ, Thy Son, help us to win the field on this earth, yea, in Him alone. Be Thou alone our Helper, protect us with Thy sword, that we may together, as Thy heroes, obtain the crown, and be forever with Thee. Amen."

—*Martyrs Mirror,* p. 430.

BIBLIOGRAPHY

The following bibliography is a brief listing of relevant sources from among many. The reading of these books enriched this study and they are submitted as further aid to the reader.

Chapter I. THE CHURCH IN MISSION

Bender, Harold S., *These Are My People,* Herald Press, Scottdale, Pa. (1961).

Graber, J. D., *The Church Apostolic,* Herald Press, Scottdale, Pa. (1960).

Latourette, K. S., *The Christian World Mission in Our Day,* Harper, New York (1954).

Miller, Donald G., *The Nature and Mission of the Church,* John Knox, Richmond, Va. (4th printing 1959).

Minear, Paul S., *Jesus and His People,* Association Press, New York (1956).

Nelson, J. Robert, *The Realm of Redemption,* Epworth Press, London (1951).

Newbigin, Lesslie, *The Household of God,* Friendship Press, New York (1954).

Yoder, John Howard, *As You Go,* Herald Press, Scottdale, Pa. (1961).

Chapter II. THE PRIMACY OF THE IN-CHRIST EXPERIENCE

Allport, Gordon, *The Individual and His Religion,* Macmillan, New York (1950).

Augsburger, Myron, *Called to Maturity,* Herald Press, Scottdale, Pa. (1960).

Homrighousen, Elmer, *Choose Ye This Day.*

Jones, E. Stanley, *Conversion,* Abingdon, New York (1959).

Nee, Watchman, *The Normal Christian Witness,* London (1958).

Sherrill, Lewis O., *The Struggle of the Soul,* Macmillan, New York (1953).

Smith, Oswald, *The Man God Uses,* Zondervan, Grand Rapids, Mich.

Stewart, James S., *A Man in Christ,* Harper, New York.

Tozer, A. W., *The Pursuit of God,* Harrisburg, Pa. (1956).

Trueblood, Elton, *The Company of the Committed,* Harper, New York (1961).

Chapter III. THE INTELLECTUAL CHALLENGE OF FAITH

Bennett, John C., *Christianity and Our World,* Hazelton Press, New York (1941).

Buber, Martin, *I and Thou,* T. & T. Clark, Edinburgh (1953).

Erb, Alta, *Christian Nurture of Children*, Herald Press, Scottdale, Pa. (1955).

Hutchinson, John, *Faith, Reason, and Existence*, Oxford Press, New York (1956).

Kierkegaard, Soren, *Training in Christianity*, Princeton, Univ. Press (1957).

Temple, Wm., *Nature, Man, and God*, Macmillan, London (1934).

Tillich, Paul, *The Courage to Be*, Yale Univ. Press, New Haven (1953).

Trueblood, Elton, *Philosophy of Religion*, Harper, New York (1957).

Chapter IV. THE THEOLOGY OF EVANGELISM

Allen, Roland, *Missionary Methods, St. Paul's and Ours*, Eerdmans, Grand Rapids, Mich. (1962 edition).

Augsburger, Myron, *Plus Living*, Zondervan, Grand Rapids, Mich. (1963).

Baily, Donald, *God Was in Christ*, Scribners, New York (1948).

Barth, Karl, *Dogmatics in Outline*, Harper, New York (1959).

Brunner, Emil, *I Believe in the Living God*, Westminster, Philadelphia (1961).

Brunner, Emil, *Our Faith*, Scribner, New York (1949).

Chafer, Lewis Sperry,*True Evangelism*, Philadelphia (1909).

Graham, Billy, *Peace with God*, Doubleday, New York (1953).

Machen, J. Gresham, *The Christian View of Man*, Eerdmans, Grand Rapids, Mich. (1937).

Morris, Leon, *The Apostolic Preaching of the Cross*, Eerdmans, Grand Rapids, Mich. (1955).

Niebuhr, Reinhold, *The Nature and Destiny of Man*, Scribner, New York.

Robinson, H. Wheeler, *The Christian Doctrine of Man*, Edinburgh (1911).

Tozer, A. W., *Of God and Men*, Christian Publications, Harrisburg (1960).

Turner, H. E. W., *The Meaning of the Cross*, Mowbray, London (1959).

Wenger, J. C., *Introduction to Theology*, Herald Press, Scottdale, Pa. (1954).

Whitesell, Favis D., *Basic New Testament Evangelism*, Zondervan, Grand Rapids, Mich. (1949).

Chapter V. THE PLACE OF ETHICS IN EVANGELISM

Beach and Niebuhr, *Christian Ethics*, Ronald Press, New York (1955).

Brunner, Emil, *The Divine Imperative*, Westminster, Philadelphia (1957).

Dodd, C. H., *The Authority of the Bible*, Harper, Torchbook, New York (1958).

Henry, Carl F. H., *Christian Personal Ethics*, Eerdmans, Grand Rapids, Mich. (1957).

Hershberger, Guy F., *The Way of the Cross in Human Relations*, Herald Press, Scottdale, Pa. (1959).

Lasserre, Jean, *War and the Gospel*, Herald Press, Scottdale, Pa. (1962).

Menninger, Karl, *Love Against Hate*, Harcourt, Brace & Co., New York (1942).

Nygren, Anders, *Agape and Eros*, Westminster, Philadelphia (1953).

Taylor, A. E., *The Faith of a Moralist*, Macmillan, New York (1930).

Chapter VI. THE CONTRIBUTION OF EVANGELISM TO CULTURE

Daniels, Robert V., *The Nature of Communism*, Random House, New York (1962).

Hostetler, John A., *The Sociology of Mennonite Evangelism*, Herald Press, Scottdale, Pa. (1954).

Kreider, Roy, *Judaism Meets Christ*, Herald Press, Scottdale, Pa. (1960).

Niebuhr, Richard, *Christ and Culture*, Harper, New York (1951).

Niebuhr, Richard, *The Kingdom of God in America*, Harper, New York.

Mennonite General Conference, *The Way of Christian Love in Race Relations*, Herald Press, Scottdale, Pa. (1955).

Northridge, W. L., *Psychology and Pastoral Practice*, Epworth, London (1953).

Chapter VII. THE MISSION OF THE LOCAL CONGREGATION

Bonhoeffer, Dietrich, *Life Together*, Harper, New York (1954).

Conant, J. E., *Every-Member Evangelism*, Harper, New York (1922).

Dean, Horace F., *Visitation Evangelism Made Practical*, Zondervan, Grand Rapids, Mich. (1957).

Golay, Eugene E., *Lay Visitation Evangelism in the Local Church*, Tidings, Nashville, Tenn. (1956).

Green, Bryan, *The Practice of Evangelism*, Scribner, New York (1955).

Littell, Franklin, *The Anabaptist View of the Church*, Starr King Press, Boston (1958).

Macaulay and Belton, *Personal Evangelism*, Moody Press, Chicago (1956).

Miller, Paul M., *Group Dynamics in Evangelism*, Herald Press, Scottdale, Pa. (1958).

Chapter VIII. THE PRIMACY OF THE SPIRIT'S ROLE

Augsburger, Myron S., *Quench Not the Spirit,* Herald Press, Scottdale, Pa. (1961).

Cattell, Everett L., *The Spirit of Holiness,* Eerdmans, Grand Rapids, Mich. (1963).

Coltman, Wm. G., *The Holy Spirit, Our Helper,* Findlay, Ohio (1946).

Lehman, Chester K., *The Holy Spirit and the Holy Life,* Herald Press, Scottdale, Pa. (1959).

Logsdon, Franklin S., *The Lord of the Harvest,* Zondervan, Grand Rapids, Mich. (1954).

Pache, Rene, *The Person and Work of the Holy Spirit,* Moody, Chicago (1954).

Ramm, Bernard, *The Witness of the Spirit,* Eerdmans, Grand Rapids, Mich. (1959).

Rees, Tom, *The Spirit of Life,* Moody, Chicago (1957).

Shoemaker, Samuel, *With the Holy Spirit and with Fire,* Harper, New York (1960).

Wilson, Dr. Walter, *The Holy Spirit and You,* Kansas City, Mo., Tract.

Chapter IX. THE VICTORY OF DEPTH PRAYER

Bounds, E. M., *The Preacher and Prayer,* Zondervan, Grand Rapids, Mich. (1946).

Buttrick, George, *Prayer,* Abingdon Press, New York (1942).

Day, Albert, *An Autobiography of Prayer,* Harper, New York (1952).

Hallesby, O., *Prayer,* Augsburg, Minneapolis (1931).

Horton, Thomas C., *The Potency of Prayer,* Revell, Westwood, N.J. (1958).

Laubach, Frank C., *Prayer, the Mightiest Force in the World,* Revell, N.J. (1956).

Rees, Paul S., *Prayer and Life's Highest,* Eerdmans, Grand Rapids, Mich. (1956).

Redpath, Alan, et al., *Prayer, Its Deeper Dimensions,* Zondervan, Grand Rapids, Mich. (1963).

Rice, John R., *Prayer, Asking and Receiving,* Wheaton, Sword of the Lord (1942).

Rinker, Rosalind, *Prayer, Conversing with God,* Zondervan, Grand Rapids, Mich. (1959).

Strong, J. Henry, *Jesus The Man of Prayer,* Judson Press, Philadelphia (1945).

Chapter X. THE STRATEGY OF CONFRONTATION

Bayly, Joseph, *The Gospel Blimp,* Windward Press, Havertown, Pa. (1960).

Burnham and Fisher, *Billy Graham and the New York Crusade,* Zondervan, Grand Rapids, Mich. (1957).

Coleman, Robert E., *The Master Plan of Evangelism,* Rusthoi, L.A., Calif. (1963).

Dean, Horace, *Operation Evangelism,* Zondervan, Grand Rapids, Mich. (1957).

Ferm, Robert O., *Persuaded to Live,* Revell, Westwood, N.J. (1958).

Green, Bryan, *The Practice of Evangelism,* Scribners, New York (1955).

McGavran, Donald, *Bridges of God,* Friendship Press, N.Y. (1955).

Miller, Donald, *Biblical Preaching,* John Knox Press, Richmond, Va.

Munro, Harry C., *Fellowship Evangelism Through Church Groups,* Bethany Press, St. Louis (1951).

Lindsell, Harold, *Missionary Principles and Practices,* Revell, Westwood, N.J. (1955).

Oates, Wayne E., *The Christian Pastor,* Westminster, Philadelphia (1951).

Sweazey, George, *Effective Evangelism,* Harper, New York (1953).

Trueblood, Elton, *The Company of the Committed,* Chapter 4.

Chapter XI. THE MODERN MAZE

Boisen, Anton T., *Religion in Crisis and Custom,* Harper, New York (1955).

Buttrick, George, *Christ and History,* Abingdon, New York (1963).

Editors of *Fortune, The Exploding Metropolis,* Doubleday, Garden City, N.Y. (1958).

Jackson, N. P., "Religion and the Fragmentation of Man," *Journal of Religion.*

Perry, Edmund, *The Gospel in Dispute,* Doubleday, Garden City, N.Y. (1958).

Rian, Edwin H., *Christianity and World Revolution,* Harper, New York (1963).

Riesman, Glazer, and Denney, *The Lonely Crowd,* Doubleday, Garden City, N.Y. (1953).

Rische, Henry, *American Youth in Trouble,* Revell, Westwood, N.J. (1957).

Templeton, Charles, *Evangelism for Tomorrow,* Harper, New York (1957).

Thielicke, Helmut, *The Freedom of the Christian Man: A Christian Confrontation with the Secular Gods,* Harper, New York (1963).

Vos, Howard F., Ed. *Religions in a Changing World,* Moody, Chicago (1959).

Whyte, Wm., *The Organization Man,* Doubleday, Garden City, N.Y. (1956).